Thomas Jefferson and the Declaration of Independence

Probably a fairly accurate representation of Jefferson's appearance in July 1776. In this detail from the Trumbull painting (see page 110), he is flanked by Sherman and Livingston (left) and by Franklin (right). (Library of Congress)

THOMAS JEFFERSON

and the

Declaration of Independence

The writing and editing of the document that marked
the birth of the United States of America

by James Munves

Charles Scribner's Sons, New York

In Memory of Anne Diven
1933-1976

ACKNOWLEDGMENTS

I would like to express my gratitude to Miss Sylvia Hilton and the staff of the New York Society Library, for their always cordial assistance; also to that other venerable and irreplaceable institution, the New-York Historical Society.

James Munves/New York, N.Y./August 11, 1976

Copyright © 1978 James Munves
Library of Congress Cataloging in Publication Data
Munves, James.
Thomas Jefferson and the Declaration of
independence.
SUMMARY: Reconstructs seventeen days in the
life of Thomas Jefferson during which the
Declaration of Independence is written and edited.
Includes reproductions of original manuscripts
showing revisions and deletions.
1. United States. Declaration of independence—
Juvenile literature. 2. Jefferson, Thomas,
Pres. U.S., 1743-1826—Juvenile literature.
[1. United States. Declaration of independence.
2. Jefferson, Thomas, Pres. U.S., 1743-1826]
I. Title.
E221.M86   973.3'13   75-39299
ISBN 0-684-14657-6 lib. bdg.

Contents

List of Illustrations

Foreword

Thomas Jefferson and the Declaration of Independence tells the story of the writing and editing of an historic document. Our main sources for reconstructing the events in this book are the Journals of the Continental Congress, notes made by Jefferson, letters written by John Adams, Jefferson, and other members of Congress, Jefferson's Rough Draft of the Declaration, copies he made for George Wythe and Richard Henry Lee, and a copy made by John Adams.

The Journals of the Continental Congress give us the dates that provide the framework of the story. Jefferson's notes tell us something about how he worked on the Declaration. Most of the story, however, is contained in the Rough Draft of the Declaration (reproduced on pages 78, 82, 86, 90). This is a remarkable document showing many stages of composition. As we shall see, the Rough Draft was not the original draft—it was copied from some earlier papers. It was, however, copied at a very early stage in the work and preserves all the changes made from that time until Jefferson submitted the Declaration to Congress. How are the different layers of changes, made at different times, to be distinguished?

Fortunately, other copies of the Declaration are preserved. One very important one, made by John Adams (see page 60), has in it only about one-fifth of the changes shown in the Rough Draft. It therefore serves as a guidepost for separating the various layers of changes. From it we can assume:

1) the changes that Adams incorporated in his copy must have been made before Adams made his copy;

2) the changes in the Rough Draft that are not incorporated in Adams's copy must have been made after Adams made his copy;

3) many words incorporated in Adams's copy are not the original words of the Rough Draft, but appear in that draft written above or over previous words that have been erased or crossed out. The crossed-out words, obviously, were written first. Therefore, by taking Adams's copy and substituting in it the crossed-out words, we can recreate the Rough Draft as it read before Jefferson made any changes. The scholar Carl Becker was the first to do this, and the author acknowledges his debt to him.

At the other end of the process, we know that the Rough Draft, with all its changes, represents the Declaration as it was worded when it was submitted to Congress. We know this because Jefferson made several copies for friends. A letter accompanying the copy he sent to Richard Henry Lee states that it is the Declaration as originally framed, that is, as submitted to Congress.

The sorting out of the authors of various changes made after Adams wrote out his copy is based on Jefferson's notes and some detective work, notably by Becker and by Professor

Julian Boyd of Princeton. Some years after writing the Declaration—perhaps when he was quite old—Jefferson actually made notations on the Rough Draft regarding the contributions of Adams and Benjamin Franklin (page 78). The accuracy of Jefferson's recollection of these contributions has been questioned. Becker and Boyd have, by logic, handwriting analysis, and examination of documents through magnifying glasses, made some educated guesses as to the extent of Franklin's editing and the order in which he and Adams saw the document. Becker thought Franklin saw it first. Boyd, whose arguments are followed in this book, believes Adams saw it first (see notes, page 130).

The following dates, preserved from history, are of significance in determining when the Declaration was written and edited:

June 7, 1776	Friday	Richard Henry Lee presents the Virginia resolution on independence to the Continental Congress.
June 11, 1776	Tuesday	Committee of Five is appointed to write the Declaration of Independence.
June 13, 1776	Thursday	George Wythe leaves Philadelphia for Virginia, taking with him the third draft of Jefferson's constitution for Virginia. The part of the *first* draft of this constitution, used by Jefferson as a basis for part of the Declaration, must have been written no later than this day.
June 18, 1776	Tuesday	Congress receives a letter from General Artemas Ward with news of the capture of a company of Scottish Highlanders. As explained in Chapter 11, page 4 of the Rough Draft, which alludes to this, could not have been copied before this date.
June 28, 1776	Friday	Jefferson presents the Declaration of Independence to the Continental Congress. He reads it aloud and it is tabled.
July 1, 1776	Monday	Lee resolution on independence is debated in Congress.
July 2, 1776	Tuesday	Lee resolution on independence is passed by Congress. Congress begins editing the Declaration of Independence.
July 3, 1776	Wednesday	Congress continues editing the Declaration of Independence.
July 4, 1776	Thursday	Congress finishes editing the Declaration of Independence and sends it to the printer.

The basis for showing Jefferson at his writing desk in the early morning comes from records of his general working habits and of the hours during which Congress was in session. We also know that little writing was done at night in that era of illumination by tallow and sperm whale oil.

James Munves

CHAPTER ONE

Writer at Work

Things have been bad in the American colonies, and they are getting worse. A hand writes on the right-hand side of a sheet of paper which has been creased down the middle:

> *and at this time are permitting their sovereign*

There is a pause. The tall quill pen, made out of a bird's feather, draws a line through two words and inserts the word "they" to provide a subject for what now has become a separate sentence.

> *they*
> ~~*and*~~ *at this time* ⌄ *are permitting their ~~sovereign~~ chief magistrate to*
> *send over not soldiers of our own blood but foreign mercenaries to destroy*
> *us*

The man holding the pen is tall and thin, with sandy hair and a freckled face. He has a long nose and a jutting chin. His name is Thomas Jefferson. The room he is working in is on the second floor of a new house on a quiet street in Philadelphia, Pennsylvania. It is early in the morning of a day in the middle of June 1776.

Jefferson has rented two rooms, a parlor and a bedroom, from the owner of the house, a bricklayer named Jacob Graff. As he works in the parlor, Jefferson hears from below the sound of a baby bawling and the clatter of pans as Mrs. Maria Graff makes her breakfast.

Jefferson has been assigned a writing task by the Continental Congress. The Congress represents thirteen of the British colonies in North America. For more than a year, Britain and these colonies have been fighting and sending messages to each other—at war, but hoping to find a way of getting together again. Now, in June 1776, Congress is trying to decide whether to break away from the mother country. It has asked Jefferson to write a paper, a declaration, explaining why the colonies seek independence. He has been working on this declaration for several days and has finished more than half of it.

He works at a small portable desk placed on a long table. Jefferson likes to do his writing in four-page folders. He makes these by taking a sheet of paper about 11″ by 14″ and folding it in half so that it makes four pages, each about 7″ by 11″. The folder is open on his desk, the left-hand side (second page) is already covered with his small, neat handwriting. He is working about half-way down on the right-hand side (third page). Many words are crossed out—the stops and starts and fits of Jefferson's trying to say exactly what he wants to say.

When Jefferson is satisfied with what he has written he will transfer the corrected version to another four-page folder which, without all the changes, will be easier to read.

Jefferson starts writing again:

> *send over not soldiers of our own blood but foreign mercenaries to destroy*
>
> *us. this is too much to be borne even by relations.*

Just a month before a frightening message had arrived in Philadelphia, telling of the plans the British were making to crush the American rebels. It mentioned: "Hessians twelve thousand, Brunswickers, Woolfenbutlers and Waldeckers five thousand." These were hired soldiers from small German states, blue-coated professionals who did not speak English, to whom the tall man at the writing desk is a nobody, a foreign devil. They would arrive on the largest British warfleet ever assembled, together with many thousands of British regulars *of our own blood*.

A thin fourteen-year-old boy, dressed in a shiny green suit and black stockings, with brass buttons on his coat and brass buckles on his shoes, enters the little second-floor parlor where Jefferson sits at his desk. The boy carries a teapot. Jefferson watches as the boy pours him a cup and fetches some wafers from a box. Jefferson sips his tea, then puts it down on the table, beside his portable writing desk:

> *and at this time* they *are permitting their* ~~sovereign~~ *chief magistrate to*
>
> *send over not soldiers of our own blood but foreign mercenaries to* ~~destroy~~ invade and
> deluge us in blood
> ~~us~~. *this is too much to be borne even by relations.*

Deluge us in blood. Jefferson nods, his mind returning to the previous winter, 1775, when the royal governor of Virginia, Lord Dunmore, had begun making war on the rebellious Virginians, raiding the colony's seaboard, leading soldiers up rivers, granting freedom to those slaves who would join his forces—the blacks in tunics emblazoned *Liberty To Slaves*. Slaves with guns were something every white man dreaded.

". . . a gentleman of thirty-two who could calculate an eclipse, survey an estate, tie an artery, plan an edifice, try a cause, break a horse, dance a minuet, and play the violin."

This description of Jefferson, from a biography written a century ago by James Parton, only partially lists Jefferson's accomplishments. He was also a mathematician, a linguist, a philosopher, an inventor, and a keen student of natural phenomena. (Independence National Historical Park Collection)

Jefferson is full of worry in Philadelphia, knowing that Patty, his dear wife, is, contrary to his wishes, down at the Virginia capes where Dunmore had been trying to start a slave rebellion. He will have more to say about the use of slaves against masters, of the guilt of the King whom Lord Dunmore serves. The question of slavery agitates Jefferson. He knows slavery is wrong, and yet he himself owns many slaves.

Jefferson, at thirty-three, possesses a mind unlike any other in the Continental Congress. There are many brilliant men in that body: eminent lawyers and students of history, philosophy, religion and government. But none has read as widely as Jefferson, or is as fluent in as many tongues. Many know Greek and Latin, but Jefferson knows French and Italian as well. Although he has never been more than a few hundred miles from his Virginia home he is already a citizen of the world. He is familiar with the new idea of the French writer and philosopher Jean Jacques Rousseau, that man is basically good. He is aware of mankind's painful history.

If other members of Congress are absorbed in the day-to-day struggle to raise and supply armies, Jefferson never loses sight of what lies ahead, of what might be. He dreams that America can become a new kind of country in which people can live free of the oppressions that have always burdened mankind.

Jefferson knows the cycle of nations. He has read of the way the vigor and freedom of a young country are lost as it becomes over-confident, rich, and powerful. As a country becomes older, its government too often gets bigger and bigger like a large fish that ends up swallowing everything else in the pond. The government in England is like that, taxing its people to pay the salaries of officials whom nobody needs, and to support armies and navies that do little good.

Jefferson dreams that if America becomes an independent nation it will somehow remain a place of freedom, where virtue and ability will be rewarded, where government will remain a servant of the people rather than become a cruel oppressor.

Always such ideas are in his mind. The colonies' virtues, he knows, rest in their youth—in the new, unspoiled conditions and opportunities he knows so well from the Virginia frontier where he had been raised. If he is fortunate to live in such a time, such good fortune has to be preserved for his children and grandchildren. The love of freedom that grows in those who have it must be kept from withering away. New forms of government, giving the people more power, more control over their government, can perhaps do this. They can also render the political soil unfit for such rank growths as an established (state-supported) church or an aristocracy based on inherited wealth.

His colony, Virginia, is even now drawing up a new government, and Jefferson is sorry he cannot be there. He has spent most of his spare time in May and early June writing his ideas for a constitution for Virginia. In his proposed constitution, the people of Virginia will be free to worship or not worship as they like, nor will any church receive money from the state. And an aristocracy will be prevented by forcing property owners to divide their estates among all their heirs. *Primogeniture*, the passing of an entire estate to the eldest son, which makes possible the perpetuation of aristocratic lines, will be outlawed in Virginia. The Virginia constitution, he is certain, will be of far more lasting importance than a congressional declaration. He wishes he could be in Williamsburg to argue for his constitution and to be closer to his wife, Patty, who is expecting a baby.

Through the open window at the far side of the room comes the voice of a fish peddler calling out his wares, then the sound of hoofbeats. The slave boy in the green suit sits cross-legged on his pallet in the corner, polishing Thomas Jefferson's boots. Jefferson begins to write again:

~~and~~ at this time ˄are permitting their ~~sovereign~~ chief magistrate to (with *they* written above ~~and~~, *are*)

send over not soldiers of our own blood but foreign mercenaries to ~~destroy~~ (with *invade and* written above ~~destroy~~)

~~us.~~ this is too much to be borne even by relations. (with *deluge us in blood* written above ~~us.~~)

He makes two additional changes on the second line:

send over not soldiers of our ~~own~~ blood but foreign mercenaries to ~~destroy~~
(above "not": *only*; above "own": *common*; above "destroy": *invade and*)

He goes on:

~~us.~~ this is too much to be borne even by relations. enough be it to say we are
(above "us.": *deluge us in blood*)
now done with them! we must endeavor to forget our former love for them
and to hold them, as the rest of mankind, enemies in war, in peace friends.
we might have been a great & a happy people together, but communicated

No, that is going the wrong way:

we might have been a great & a happy people together, but communicat~~ed~~ion of happiness
(above the insertion: *a*)
& of grandeur it seems is beneath their dignity.

No:

& of grandeur it seems is be~~neath~~ their dignity. we will climb then the roads to glory &
(above "neath": *low*)
happiness apart be it so, since they will have it.

There is something he doesn't like. He reads over what he has just written. The order is wrong. First put in the agreement, *be it so* (have it your way), then say we will go our own way.

& of grandeur it seems is be~~neath~~ their dignity. ~~we will climb then the roads to glory &~~
(above "neath": *low*)
~~happiness apart~~ be it so, since they will have it. the road to glory & to happiness
is open to us too, we will climb it in a separate state & acquiesce in the necessity
which pronounces our everlasting Adieu.

That is what this is all about, the *everlasting Adieu* of the colonies to Great Britain. He must remember to call them *states* now. *States.* Things are changing swiftly in Philadelphia in the middle of June 1776.

5

CHAPTER TWO

Bad News in May

Six months earlier, at the end of December 1775, Jefferson had left Philadelphia for his home in Virginia. There had still been hopes, then, of making peace with Britain. In July 1775, the Continental Congress had sent a petition, a formal written request, to King George III in the hope that he would prefer the "olive branch" of peace to the sword of war. The Congress thought that the King would see that it would be foolish to fight the colonies. The American general Richard Montgomery had just taken Montreal, and the capture of Quebec was expected. Once Quebec fell, Congress expected that Canada would join the other thirteen colonies in the rebellion and that the King would see that he could not defeat the colonists by force of arms.

Jefferson had returned to Philadelphia on May 14, 1776, to find a different spirit. Not only had the King not answered the Olive Branch Petition, he had declared the colonies out of his protection and ordered a naval blockade. And the Canadian campaign had turned into a disaster.

On May 15, 1776, the day after Jefferson's return, Congress, which had already told the thirteen colonies to form state governments of their own, instructed that all signs and instruments of the King's authority be suppressed. With that act, the United Colonies had become independent in all but name.

That same day, May 15, the *Pennsylvania Gazette* had published a dispatch from Hamburg (dated February 6, 1776) about the hiring of German troops by Colonel Faucitt, agent of the British Crown. Then, five days later, on May 20, a spy had brought Congress the British war plans against the colonies and the actual treaties by which the British had hired soldiers from the German princes of Hesse-Cassel, Brunswick, Hesse-Hanau, Anspach-Bayreuth, Waldeck, and Anhalt-Zerbst. The plans and treaties had been sent by Arthur Lee, a Virginia-born British lawyer. Arthur and his brother William, a London alderman, were sympathetic to the colonies. Their brother, Richard Henry Lee, was a Virginia delegate to the Continental Congress.

The British planned to have 30,000 troops in America by June. Arthur Lee had written:

> . . . there is not a power in this quarter of the globe that
> has not been applied to either to take an active part
> against or at least to withhold assistance from you . . .
> 'tis certain the French will not openly interfere in your
> behalf 'till you avow an independence.
> In short, the plan . . . is as early as possible to attack you
> in various parts with the whole force of the country. If
> you are conquered, besides hanging and confiscations un-
> numerable, the remaining poor souls will be worse slaves
> than Mexico or Peru. . . . There is no alternative but an
> instant avowal of independence & a consequent negotia-
> tion, at least for naval alliance. . . .

The spy who had brought the papers from Arthur Lee was George Merchant, another Virginian. Merchant had been serving in the American army when he was captured by the British during the ill-fated Canadian campaign of the previous winter. He had been shipped to England in chains to be executed. He had been rescued from jail by the Lord Mayor of London who, like many other Britons, sympathized with the Americans, and by Alderman William Lee, Arthur Lee's brother. George Merchant had been sent home with the messages cunningly sewn in the waistband of his breeches.

Yet on this mid-June day, as Thomas Jefferson worked at his desk, his stockinged heels resting on the freshly sanded floor, Pennsylvania and three other colonies still had royal governors. Congress's instructions still had not been acted on. The royal coat of arms and portraits and monuments of the King were everywhere. And they were all, every last colonist—whether a buckskin-clad hunter in the mountains or a velvet-and-lace-garbed delegate to the Continental Congress—British subjects.

The papers accrediting Jefferson as a member of the Congress had been issued by

> a General Assembly begun and held at the Capitol in the
> city of Williamsburg on Thursday, the first day of June,
> *in the fifteenth Year of the Reign of our Lord GEORGE*
> *the third, by the Grace of God, of Great Britain, France*
> *and Ireland, King*, defender of the Faith, &c. Annoque
> Domini 1775 . . .

As British subjects, all the members of the Congress called to Philadelphia to offer a united resistance to Britain were traitors. Especially singled out were the president of Congress, John Hancock, his fellow Massachusetts colleagues John and Samuel Adams, and Thomas Jefferson. They were to be excluded from any acts of pardon and amnesty that might later excuse other Americans.

7

If captured, they would be dragged to the gallows and

> hanged by the neck, but not until you are dead; for, while you are still living your bodies are to be taken down, your bowels torn out and burned before your faces, your heads then cut off, and your bodies divided each into four quarters, and your heads and quarters to be then at the King's disposal . . .

Such was the penalty for those who defied their monarch. It had been carried out, just one year before, against some rebels in Ireland.

Independence, barely whispered in Congress in 1774 and 1775, had emerged as an issue in 1776, following the publication in January of Thomas Paine's pamphlet *Common Sense*, and the news, shortly after, that Parliament had put the colonies out of its protection—in effect, declared war on them.

Common Sense loosened loyalty to the King—the basis of monarchy—in a clever way. It pitted a religious authority—the Bible—against the religious reverence for the King. The British people, like other Europeans, had been taught to think of their King (who was the head of the Anglican Church as well as the head of state) as ruling by "divine right." Obedience to the King was the subject's duty. Disobedience was a sin. Paine cleverly quoted the Old Testament, sacred to the Protestant dissenters who had settled America, to show that kings and their hereditary succession were not inevitable. He used biblical arguments to demonstrate that the Jews had governed themselves before the days of Saul, David, and Solomon; and he ridiculed the extravagance and stupidity of monarchs. A hundred thousand copies of *Common Sense*, purchased by a literate population of a million, prepared a lot of minds for what was coming.

Events had just unfolded. The colonists had said *no* to the King's taxes and to laws that ruined colonial merchants. Then, in April 1775, at Lexington and Concord, they had had to fire at the King's soldiers to make good their word. One act led to another. Men who had grown up helping run churches, towns, and colonies now sat in Philadelphia trying to manage a vast area four times the size of Britain, making war on the strongest empire in the world. They did not have a proper government. No one was in charge. All the work was done by committees. Working committees dealt with lesser matters; more important business was handled by fourteen standing committees, which included the equivalent of a War Department, a Navy Department, and a Treasury. Another committee engaged in secret negotiations with France. The colonies' enemy in the recent French and Indian War now seemed interested in helping them against its bitter enemy, England.

The delegates to the Continental Congress were legislators and administrators all in one. The more they did, the less they feared to attempt. What could they not do?

CHAPTER THREE

A Resolution in June

Independence moved to center stage on Friday, June 7, 1776, when one of Virginia's delegates to the Continental Congress presented a three-part resolution that had been forwarded from Williamsburg on May 15. The resolution was presented by delegate Richard Henry Lee, brother of Arthur Lee and William Lee of London. Its first part went:

> RESOLVED unanimously, that the delegates appointed to represent this colony in General Congress be instructed to propose that respectable body to declare the United Colonies free and independent states, absolved from all allegiance to, or dependence upon, the crown or parliament of Great Britain . . .

Before presenting the resolution to Congress, however, Lee reworded it. Ten years before, the British Parliament had declared that the colonies

> have been, are, and of right ought to be subordinate unto, and dependent upon the imperial crown and parliament of *Great Britain.* . . .

Remembering this, Lee changed the first part of the resolution so that it mocked the British declaration:

> Resolved that these United Colonies are, and of right ought to be, free and independent States, that they are absolved from all allegiance to the British Crown . . .

Congress had a way of talking about issues to test opinion without taking an official vote. Once Congress voted, its decision was final. With an issue as important as independence, a vote taken too soon could destroy the Congress. Colonies

Richard Henry Lee, eloquent advocate of independence, was the seventh of eleven children of a prosperous Virginia planter. He was educated in England. His left hand was crippled when a gun burst while he was hunting swans. (Portrait by Charles Willson Peale, National Portrait Gallery, Smithsonian Institution, Washington, D.C.)

that disagreed with the majority decision might leave. To be safe, Congress would turn itself into a Committee of the Whole, which would *advise* Congress on what to do. The advice of the committee, unlike the vote of a majority of Congress, did not have to be followed. No colony would leave Congress because of a mere recommendation, whatever it was.

When Congress became a Committee of the Whole, President John Hancock stepped down, and Benjamin Harrison of Virginia took the chair as head of the committee. Everyone else stayed where he was, but now everything that happened took place in the Committee of the Whole rather than in Congress.

The Committee of the Whole argued about independence all day Saturday, June 8, and most of the following Monday, June 10. John Dickinson of Pennsylvania, Robert Livingston of New York, Edward Rutledge of South Carolina, and others said that the colonists were not yet ready for independence. They believed that if Congress did something that the people did not agree with, the people would not support the action. If the colonies were not really *united* as they claimed to be, no other nation would make a treaty with them. And without a treaty of alliance with a powerful country like France, the colonies would have no chance of winning the war.

Resolved   ~~the may to yay~~   11

That these United Colonies are, and of
right ought to be, free and independent States, that
they are absolved from all allegiance to the British
Crown, and that all political connection between them
and the State of Great Britain is, and ought to be,
totally dissolved.

That it is expedient forthwith to take the
most effectual measures for forming foreign
alliances.

That a plan of confederation be prepared
and transmitted to the respective Colonies for
their consideration and approbation.

The resolution on Independence in Richard Henry Lee's own hand. (Library of
Congress)

Two Massachusetts delegates, Sam Adams and his cousin John Adams, argued that the people in the colonies were ahead of Congress in their desire for independence. Sam Adams, who rarely spoke in Congress, made a strong impression. As a member of the Massachusetts Committee of Correspondence he had read many letters from committees in the other colonies. For example, he said, he had many letters and documents to show that the people of North Carolina were very eager for independence. As he talked quietly and confidently, rising on his toes as he ended a telling sentence, one delegate from that colony who had been full of doubt threw up his hands. "It is done," exclaimed Joseph Hewes of North Carolina. "I will abide by it."

Sam Adams was very convincing. One Pennsylvania delegate, John Morton, who up to then had agreed with Dickinson, began wondering who was right. But still, when the Committee of the Whole voted, only seven of the thirteen colonies were found to be in favor of recommending independence. This was a majority, enough to carry a motion for independence. But what if the six colonies not in favor did not join the seven in forming a new nation? It was safer not to do anything for the moment. A motion by Edward Rutledge that Congress not vote on independence for three weeks was passed by a vote of 7 to 5.

Meanwhile, so that not too much time would be lost by the delay, three committees were set up to make preparations for independence. One committee was to make foreign alliances; the second was to plan a new government for the thirteen colonies; and the third was to write a declaration explaining to the world why the colonies wanted independence.

Richard Henry Lee, who had introduced the independence resolution, should have been elected to the five-man committee to write the Declaration. He was, however, unpopular with the Virginia delegation because he had, as a member of the Virginia legislature, led an investigation that exposed the shady financial dealings of several members. Jefferson, the youngest member of the delegation, was elected in his place.

The other four members of the committee were John Adams of Massachusetts, Benjamin Franklin of Pennsylvania, Roger Sherman of Connecticut and Robert R. Livingston of New York. Sherman, a very able politician, had no writing ability. Robert Livingston, as one of those who favored delaying independence, could not have been expected to put his heart into writing a declaration. Adams and Franklin both had a lot of writing experience but neither relished writing for Congress. Besides, Adams was probably the busiest member of Congress and Franklin was ill and out of the city.

The committee, except for Franklin, probably met at least once and discussed in a general way what the Declaration ought to contain. The task of actually drafting it fell to Jefferson.

CHAPTER FOUR

The First Three Pages

When he had started to write the Declaration, probably sometime between Wednesday, June 12, and Saturday, June 15, Jefferson knew what he must do. First he had to list all the bad and unjust things the King and Parliament had done to the colonies: trying to make them obey unfair laws, making it difficult for them to govern themselves, and making war on them. Most of the Declaration would consist of charges accusing the King and Parliament of these wrongs before the world as a jury.

But under what law were the King and Parliament to be charged? It could not be under their own law, under the British constitution, because the British would argue that they had been following it. People of another nation, reading the Declaration, could not be expected to understand the intricacies of British law. They wouldn't know who was right and would only shake their heads and say that the dispute was between Britons in England and Britons in America. No. If King and Parliament were to be accused before the world, the colonies would have to stand outside the British constitution. They would have to make their appeal under another kind of law.

Searching history books and law books, the colonists had found this other law in the works of an English philosopher, John Locke. Almost a hundred years before, Locke had justified another rebellion, in which Britons had kicked out King James II, by inventing a new kind of law he called *natural law*.

Natural law, Locke said, was older than the British constitution. In his *Two Treatises on Civil Government*, he wrote that since men were:

> by Nature free, equal and independent, no one can be
> put out of his Estate, and subjected to the Political Power
> of another, without his own *Consent* . . .

In 1775 and 1776, natural law had become the very nerve of the American rebellion as colonies, towns, and counties used it to justify their defiance. The papers were full of statements and declarations. On June 6, 1776, the *Pennsylvania Evening Post* had published some principles that the Virginian George Mason was proposing for his state's constitution. The first paragraph of Mason's Declaration of Rights for Virginia stated:

> That all men are born equally free and independent and
> have certain inherent natural rights of which they can
> not by any compact, deprive or divest their posterity:
> among which are the enjoyment of life and liberty, with
> the means of acquiring and possessing property, and pre-
> serving and obtaining happiness and safety.

On June 12, the day after Jefferson was assigned the task of writing the Declaration for Congress, the *Pennsylvania Gazette* published Mason's declaration in its final form. At the end of the first paragraph, one word had been changed. The expression *preserving and obtaining happiness and safety* had become *pursuing and obtaining happiness and safety.*

Jefferson used these natural law arguments on the first page of the Declaration in order to show the world that the war was not a mere struggle between two groups of Englishmen. He had to show that Americans were fighting for certain basic ideas of what was right, basic ideas that were important not only to Americans but to all people everywhere.

Right: *The text of the original draft of the first page of the Declaration, reconstructed by removing changes from a later draft called the Rough Draft (see page 78).*

Jefferson's drafts of the earliest stages of the Declaration have been lost. But if the changes are removed from the Rough Draft, as we have done here, and the original words restored (by referring to the copy John Adams made at an early stage) we can see how it must have looked when Jefferson first copied it from his work sheets. This is one of the first times that the words United States of America appeared in place of United Colonies of America.
Jefferson had his own rules of spelling and punctuation. He usually spelled independant with an a (line 3) and didn't bother starting sentences with capital letters unless they began a paragraph. Shewn (line 18) was a common English spelling of shown. Some words have shifted meanings since the eighteenth century. Distinguished was then used to mean definite (line 21).

A Declaration of the Representatives of the
UNITED STATES OF AMERICA, *in General Congress assembled.*

1   When in the course of human events it becomes necessary for a people to

2   advance from that subordination in which they have hitherto remained, & to as-

3   -sume among the powers of the earth the equal & independant station to

4   which the laws of nature & of nature's god entitle them, a decent respect

5   to the opinions of mankind requires that they should declare the causes

6   which impel them to the change.

7   We hold these truths to be sacred & undeniable; that all men are

8   created equal & independant, that from that equal creation they derive

9   rights inherent & inalienable, among which are the preservation of

10   life, & liberty & the pursuit of happiness; that to secure these ends, go-

11   -vernments are instituted among men, deriving their just powers from

12   the consent of the governed; that whenever any form of government

13   shall become destructive of these ends, it is the right of the people to alter

14   or to abolish it, & to institute new government, laying it's foundation on

15   such principles & organising it's powers in such form, as to them shall

16   seem most likely to effect their safety & happiness. prudence indeed

17   will dictate that governments long established should not be changed for

18   light & transient causes: and accordingly all experience hath shewn that

19   mankind are more disposed to suffer while evils are sufferable, than to

20   right themselves by abolishing the forms to which they are accustomed. but

21   when a long train of abuses & usurpations, begun at a distinguished period,

22   & pursuing invariably the same object, evinces a design to subject

23   them to arbitrary power, it is their right, it is their duty, to throw off such

24   government & to provide new guards for their future security. such has

25   been the patient sufferance of these colonies; & such is now the necessity

26   which constrains them to expunge their former systems of government.

27   the history of his present majesty, is a history of unremitting injuries and

28   usurpations, among which no one fact stands single or solitary to contra-

29   -dict the uniform tenor of the rest, all of which have in direct object the

30   establishment of an absolute tyranny over these states. to prove this, let facts be

31   submitted to a candid world, for the truth of which we pledge a faith

32   yet unsullied by falsehood.

When it came to the specific charges against the King, Jefferson had a list that he had already prepared for his preamble to the Virginia Constitution. For the time being, he kept these charges separate, so that the first draft of the Declaration of Independence was in two parts. Jefferson had the four-page folder and the sheet with the charges. He would put them together later.

On that morning in mid-June he was, as we have seen, working on the third page of the four-page folder. He was writing the next-to-the-last paragraph, studying it on the inclined surface of his portable desk, as his young valet-slave Bob Hemings poured him another cup of tea. The morning sun streamed through the two east windows of the second-floor parlor. A clock attached to the side of the State House, four blocks away, tolled seven. Jefferson dipped pen into inkwell without a glance. The room was silent except for the scratching of pen on paper.

they
~~*this conduct and*~~ *at this time are permitting their ~~sovereign~~ chief magistrate to*

only common invade and
send over not soldiers of our ~~own~~ blood but foreign mercenaries to ~~destroy~~

deluge us in blood.
~~us.~~ this is too much to be borne even by relations. enough be it to say we are

now done with them! we must endeavor to forget our former love for them

and to hold them, as the rest of mankind, enemies in war, in peace friends.

a
we might have been a great & a happy people together, but communicat~~ed~~ion of happiness

low
& of grandeur it seems is be~~neath~~ their dignity. ~~we will climb then the roads to glory &~~

~~happiness apart~~ be it so, since they will have it. the road to ~~glory & to~~ happiness

is open to us too, we will climb it in a separate state, & acquiesce in the necessity

which pronounces our everlasting Adieu.

The third and fourth sentences were weak. Of course being invaded was *too much to be borne*, but couldn't he put it better? He wrote on the bottom of the page:

these facts have given the last stab to agonizing affection & manly spirit bids
us to renounce for ever these unjust brethren.

Then he made one more change:

unfeeling
us to renounce for ever these ~~unjust~~ brethren.

Now he substituted this for the original second and third sentences:

they
~~this conduct and~~ at this time ˄ are permitting their ~~sovereign~~ chief magistrate to

only   common   invade and
send over not ˄ soldiers of our ~~own~~ blood but foreign mercenaries to ~~destroy~~

deluge us in blood. these facts have given the last stab to agonizing affection & manly spirit bids us to
~~us. this is too much to be borne even by relations. enough be it to say we are~~

renounce for ever these unfeeling brethren.
~~now done with them!~~ we must endeavor to forget our former love for them

The passage still was not right:

very   too they
~~this conduct and~~ at this ˄ time ˄ are permitting their ~~sovereign~~ chief magistrate to

only   common   invade and
send over not ˄ soldiers of our ~~own~~ blood but foreign mercenaries to ~~destroy~~

deluge us in blood. these facts have given the last stab to agonizing affection & manly spirit bids us to
~~us. this is too much to be borne even by relations. enough be it to say we are~~

renounce for ever these unfeeling brethren.
~~now done with them!~~ we must endeavor to forget our former love for them

we hold
and to hold them, as ˄ the rest of mankind, enemies in war, in peace friends.

free   great   a   grandeur
we might have been a ~~great~~ & a ~~happy~~ people together, but ˄ communicat~~ed~~ion of ~~happiness~~

freedom   low
& of ~~grandeur~~ it seems is be~~neath~~ their dignity. ~~we will climb then the roads to glory &~~

~~happiness apart~~ be it so, since they will have it. the road to ~~glory & to~~ happiness
is open to us too, we will climb it in a separate state, & acquiesce in the necessity
which pronounces our everlasting Adieu.

As much as Jefferson labored to make his words flow without losing clarity and meaning, indeed to sharpen meaning, he knew that they could not be final. The four other members of his committee, then the entire Congress, would review and change them.

an authentic picture in possession of the Publishers   J. Rog

The Pennsylvania State House, where Congress met and voted for independence
(from an old engraving). (The Historical Society of Pennsylvania)

CHAPTER FIVE

The Continental Congress

Someone knocked on the door of the second-floor parlor. Bob Hemings admitted Byrne the barber, who proceeded to shave Jefferson and dress his hair. When Byrne was finished, the young valet helped Jefferson put on his boots, then went downstairs and across the street to Hiltzheimer's stables. Bob walked straight, proud of the new clothes his master had bought him in the big city. He was a light-skinned youth with a green ribbon neatly tied around his long black pigtail.

Bob saddled the two horses his master kept at Hiltzheimer's. It was half past seven. Jefferson, a tall gangly figure in fawn-colored coat and breeches, mounted his horse and rode with his valet two blocks south to Walnut Street. The big hospital building brooded in the distance, beyond the potter's field. To the east, beyond their left shoulders, the bulk of Philadelphia stood.

Philadelphia, with 34,000 souls, was the second largest city in the British Empire, bigger than Dublin or Edinburgh. It was a port between the sea and a dark interior that reached the Alleghenies and the Great Lakes. It was a welcoming place alive with people of a dozen faiths and tongues.

Jefferson's steed turned left on Walnut Street, stepping daintily around some pigs that ran across its path to grunt and root in a pile of garbage. Passing between the new prison and the high brick wall enclosing the State House yard, Jefferson and Bob Hemings were heading toward the river where masts loomed like a leafless forest over the city rooftops. Jefferson held his breath as they passed Dock Creek, an open sewer running into the Delaware River. They rode along the wharves to see what new ships had come in, then turned back to Second Street and Smith's Tavern.

Hurrying through the crowd in front of the tavern to a private room in back, Jefferson joined the committee on spies: John Adams, Edward Rutledge, James Wilson of Pennsylvania and Robert Livingston. After breakfast and a long discus-

Charles Thomson, Secretary of Congress. Born in County Derry, Ireland, he was set ashore in Delaware in 1739, at the age of ten, one of six children who'd just been orphaned by the death of their father at sea. Thomson became a prosperous Philadelphia merchant and a revolutionary leader. He was appointed Secretary of Congress by delegates from other colonies who resented the fact that the conservative Pennsylvania legislature had not named him a delegate. (Independence National Historical Park Collection)

sion on punishments for aiding the enemy, the committee went over to Chestnut Street and the State House.

With a great stir, a glittering carriage, emblazoned with a coat of arms, drew up before the long brick building. A liveried servant jumped to the ground and opened the door, while another helped the passenger down the step to the street.

The passenger emerged, attired in blue velvet, lace, ruffled cuffs and shirt front, a broad blue hat to match his waistcoat, and a polished walking stick. This was John Hancock, the richest man in Boston and president of the Continental Congress. Jefferson followed him in, climbing a few steps to enter the building, turning left to the large room in which Congress met.

A thin scholarly Irishman with the kind of face that focused sharply on what was immediately before it sat at the desk on the platform at the far end of the room. This was Charles Thomson, Secretary of Congress. He stood up as Hancock seated himself opposite, to face the other delegates. In contrast to the elegant president, Thomson dressed in plain brown patriotic homespun. He was small in his movements where Hancock was large and flamboyant.

Thomson opened a folder and handed Hancock a pile of letters that had arrived on the afternoon of the previous day. Congress was ready to begin. Hancock looked at the first letter and began reading, while Thomson, with pen poised at his journal, turned in his seat from time to time to watch the delegates.

The letters contained reports from General Washington, requests for arms and other supplies from Committees of Safety in the different colonies, and bills from cartmen for transporting army baggage. In one of his dispatches, Washington enclosed a letter, from General Artemas Ward in Massachusetts, announcing the capture of a shipload of Scottish highlanders. The army of invasion was close to America's shores! While Hancock's voice droned on, Jefferson slipped away from

Left, overleaf: *First page (preamble) of the first draft of a proposed constitution for Virginia, in Jefferson's own hand* (Library of Congress). Right, overleaf: *Type-set reconstruction*

Jefferson kept the first page of his first draft of a model Virginia constitution to use as a basis for the charges against the King, which would become the second page and part of the third page of the Declaration. The numerals along the left-hand margin show how he planned to change the order of the charges. When he wrote the Declaration, he would place the fourteenth and thirteenth charges of the preamble between numbers 10 and 11, and would put number 16 before number 10.

Guelph (line 1) means a member of a German princely family. Notice that Jefferson originally had put for imposing taxes on us without our consent *on the second line of the ninth charge, before moving it to become item (c).*

The notation &c—murders, *in item (a) of the ninth charge, refers to* protecting (the King's troops) by a mock-trial for any murders they should commit on the inhabitants of these states *(see lines 30 and 31 of the second page of the Rough Draft, page 82).*

Whereas George — Guelph king of Great Britain & Ireland and

Elector of Hanover, heretofore entrusted with the exercise of the kingly office in this government

hath endeavored to pervert the same into a detestable & insupportable tyranny

1. by putting his negative on laws the most wholesome & necessary for the public good

2. by denying to his governors permission to pass laws of immediate & pressing importance, unless suspended in their operation for his assent, & when so suspended,

neglecting to attend to them for many years:

3. by refusing to pass certain other laws, unless the persons to be benefited by them would relinquish the inestimable rights of representation in the legislature

4. by dissolving legislative assemblies repeatedly & continually for opposing with manly firmness his invasions on the rights of the people:

5. when dissolved, by refusing to call others for a long space of time, thereby leaving the political system without any legislative body head.

6. by endeavoring to prevent the population of our country & for that purpose obstructing the laws for encouraging the importation naturalization of foreigners & raising the conditions of new appropriations of lands:

7. by keeping among us in times of peace standing armies & ships of war:

8. by affecting to render the military independent of & superior to the civil power:

9. by combining with others to subject us to a foreign jurisdiction giving his assent to their pretended acts of legislation

a. for quartering large bodies of armed troops among us & protecting them &c. — murders

b. for cutting off our trade with all parts of the world

c. for imposing taxes on us without our consent

d. for depriving us of the benefits of trial by jury:

e. for transporting us beyond seas to be tried for pretended offences.

f. for suspending our own legislatures & declaring themselves invested with power to legislate for us in all cases whatsoever

10. by plundering our seas, ravaging our coasts, burning our towns, & destroying the lives of our people:

11. by inciting insurrections of our fellow subjects with the allurements of forfeiture & confiscation

12. by prompting our negroes to rise in arms among us; those very negroes whom he hath refused us permission to exclude by law:

13. by endeavoring to bring on the inhabitants of our frontiers the merciless Indian savages whose known rule of warfare is an undistinguished destruction of all ages, sexes, & conditions

14. by transporting at this time a large army of foreign mercenaries to compleat the works of death, desolation, & tyranny already begun with circumstances of cruelty so unworthy the head of a civilized nation

15. by answering our repeated petitions for redress with a repetition of injuries:

16. and finally by abandoning the helm of government & declaring us out of his allegiance & protection

and by various other acts of tyranny too often enumerated to need repetition, and too

by which several acts of misrule the said George Guelph hath forfeited the kingly office and has rendered it necessary for the preservation of the people that he should be immediately deposed from the same kingly

office & divested of all it's privileges, powers, & prerogatives:

And forasmuch as the public liberty may be more effectually secured by abolishing an office which all experience hath shewn to be inveterately inimical thereto and it will thence become further necessary to re-establish such antient principles as are friendly to the rights of the people & to declare certain others which may co-operate with & fortify the same in future

Whereas George   Guelph king of Great Britain and Ireland and
Elector of Hanover, heretofore entrusted with the exercise of the kingly office in this government
hath endeavored to pervert the same into a detestable and insupportable tyranny

1. by putting his negative on laws the most wholesome & necessary for ye. public good
   ~~had kept some colonies without judiciary establishments~~

2. by denying to his governors permission to pass laws of ~~the most~~ immediate & pressing im-
                                                                    as
   -portance, unless suspended in their operation for his ~~consent~~, and when so suspended,
   neglecting ~~for nn~~ to attend to them for many years;

3. by refusing to pass certain other laws, unless the persons to be benefited by them would
   relinquish the inestimable rights of representation in the legislature;

4. by dissolving legislative assemblies repeatedly and continually for opposing with manly firm-
   -ness his invasions on the rights of the people;

5. when dissolved, by refusing to call others for a long space of time, thereby leaving the poli-
   -tical system [~~in a state of dissolution~~] without any legislative head;

                                                    & for that purpose
6. by endeavouring to prevent the population of our country by obstructing the laws [for the
   encouraging the importation   *new*   *ons ~~new~~ of*
   naturalization] of foreigners & raising the conditions of ᐱappropriating lands;
   refused judiciary establmts . . .
   judges dependant
   erected swarms of offices

7. by keeping among us, in times of peace, standing armies & ships of war;

8. by affecting to render the military independent of & superior to the civil power;

                                                                        as
9. by combining with others to subject us to a foreign jurisdiction, giving his ~~consent~~ to
   their pretended acts of legislation ~~for imposing taxes on us without our consent~~

                                                    g
   a. for quartering large bodies of troops among us: & protect them &c—murders
   b. for cutting off our trade with all parts of the world;
   c. for ~~depriving us~~ imposing taxes on us without our consent;
   d. for depriving us of the benefits of trial by jury;
   e. for transporting us beyond seas to be tried for pretended offences;
      for taking away our charters & altering fundamentally the forms of our government
   f. for suspending our own legislatures & declaring themselves invested with power
      to legislate for us in all cases whatsoever;

16.

10. by plundering our seas, ravaging our coasts, burning our towns and destroying the lives
    of our people;

14. 13.

                        citizens
11. by inciting insurrections of our fellow ~~subjects~~ with allurement of forfeiture & confiscation
                                                        by an inhuman use of his negative
12. by prompting our negroes to rise in arms among us; those very negroes whomᐱhe hath ~~from time~~
    ~~to time~~ refused us permission to exclude by law:

13. by endeavoring to bring on the inhabitants of our frontiers the merciless Indian savages
                                                        of existence ~~of life~~
    whose known rule of warfare is undistinguished destruction of all ages, sexes & conditionsᐱ

14. by transporting at this time a large army of foreign mercenaries to compleat the works of
                        with circumstances of cruelty & perfidy   *nation*
    death, desolation, & tyranny already begun in a stile so unworthy the head of a civilized ~~people~~
                        for redress with a repetition of
15. by answering our repeated petitions ~~against this repeated~~ injuryies; ~~with a repetition of injuries~~

16. and finally by abandoning the helm of government & declaring us out of his allegiance &
    protection

his desk and went to the little library attached to the meeting room. Something about his list of charges bothered him.

Lists of charges against the King had been a feature of numerous declarations and documents issued by the colonies and Congress, and sent to other colonies in the West Indies, to Canada, and to the people of Ireland and Great Britain.

Jefferson had had little trouble in writing his list. He had used the first page of the "model Virginia constitution" which he had just written. It was called the *preamble* and was an introductory section, intended to state the facts that made it necessary to have a new constitution. These facts were in the form of a list of charges against King George, showing that he had governed badly. Jefferson had worked two references to slavery (charges 1 and 12) into the Virginia preamble. The first charge referred to the King's veto of a law that Virginia had passed to end the importation of slaves. Jefferson planned to insert the same two charges into the Declaration, but that would not be enough. He stared at the papers, gathered them up, and returned to his desk in the meeting room.

Dinner, the big meal of the day, was at four in the afternoon, after Congress adjourned.

Before going back to Smith's Tavern, Jefferson rode down Chestnut Street to Aitken's, to see what new books had come in. He was always looking for new volumes for his library. What he liked most about the city was its shops. There was nothing like them in Virginia. In Philadelphia, he would discover books, papers, maps he had never heard of; find window shutter rings, sash bolts, and spring locks for the house he was building at Monticello; and purchase gloves, hats and other things for his friends in Virginia who sent him off with shopping lists to fill.

After a long dinner with several friends, Jefferson saw John Adams briefly at a committee that had been receiving secret messages from England, and returned to the Graffs' brick house on Seventh Street.

CHAPTER SIX

Finishing the Last Two Pages

The next day, Jefferson awoke in the dark of morning as was his habit. Bob Hemings, having heard him stir, came into the bedroom with a large pitcher of cold water, which he poured into a basin on the floor. Jefferson soaked his feet in cold water every morning, a ritual that he believed ensured good health. Then Bob, who had laid out his master's clothes the night before, helped him dress. By now the first rosy flush of dawn had appeared. It was shortly after five, with just enough light in the sky to read by, when Jefferson entered the parlor and seated himself at the desk.

He had been making slight changes in the charges in his preamble to the Virginia constitution to make them fit the Declaration of Independence. He had also been rearranging their order. The twelfth charge in the Virginia preamble,

> by prompting our negroes to rise in arms among us; those
> very negroes whom by an inhuman use of his negative
> he hath refused us permission to exclude by law:

had become the fifteenth charge in the Declaration:

> he has prompted our negroes to rise in arms among us;
> those very negroes whom by an inhuman use of his nega-
> tive he hath refused us permission to exclude by law;

As he reread the charge at his desk, Jefferson was not satisfied. Unable to decide what else to say, he picked up the four-page folder and reread the first page: *When in the course of human events....* He returned to the charges. Slavery was his nightmare, darkening his dreams of the future, making him uncomfortable about the present. Jefferson had called on John Locke's natural law to justify disobedience to the Crown (*Men being . . . by Nature free, equal and independent*), yet he denied this natural law on his own plantations. He complained that King and Parliament sought to reduce him to slavery, yet the sweat of blacks afforded him time to read, study languages, and play the violin—and indeed brought the colonies much of the wealth with which they resisted the British Empire.

Well, it was not entirely his fault. He, and other Virginians like him, had been born into mastery—the sons of fathers who owned slaves inherited from their fathers before them. Someday it would have to stop. Meanwhile, Virginians sought to ease their consciences by preventing the importation of more slaves. But the King would not let them. As Jefferson had pointed out two years earlier in his first long political essay:

> The abolition of domestic slavery is the great object of desire in these colonies where it was unhappily introduced in their infant state. But previous to the enfranchisement of the slaves we have, it is necessary to exclude all further importations from Africa. Yet our repeated attempts to effect this by prohibitions, and by imposing duties which might amount to prohibition, have been hitherto defeated by his majesty's negative . . .

This was expressed in the very first of the Virginia preamble's charges:

> by putting his negative on laws the most wholesome & necessary for ye. public good

In the preamble's twelfth charge (it had become the fifteenth in the Declaration's) Jefferson blamed the King for supplying the slaves with arms to rebel. He had a great deal more to say on the subject. He crossed out the fifteenth charge and began writing rapidly, ridding himself of demons while young Bob Hemings slept on his pallet in the corner, his arms crossed over his eyes. John Wayles, Patty's father, had passed all the Hemingses on to Patty when he died, along with 128 other slaves. Bob Hemings was John Wayles's son by his half-white house slave Betty Hemings. Bob Hemings was Patty's half-brother. So he was Jefferson's half-brother-in-law, as well as his slave and his valet.

After many corrections, Jefferson finally wrote:

> *he has waged cruel war against human nature itself, violating it's*
>
> *most sacred rights of life & liberty in the persons of a distant people*

who never offended him, captivating & carrying them into slavery in another hemisphere, or to incur miserable death in their transportation thither. this piratical warfare, the opprobrium of infidel powers, is the warfare of the Christian king of Great Britain. determined to keep open a market where MEN should be bought & sold, he has prostituted his negative for suppressing every legislative attempt to prohibit or to restrain this execrable commerce: and that this assemblage of horrors might want no fact of distinguished die, he is now exciting those very people to rise in arms among us, and to purchase that liberty of which he has deprived them, by murdering the people upon whom he also obtruded them; thus paying off former crimes committed against the liberties of one people, with crimes which he urges them to commit against the lives of another.

He had taken as much time with this one charge as with all the rest.

Left, overleaf: *Type reconstruction of first page (preamble) of first draft of a proposed constitution for Virginia.* Right, overleaf: *Reconstruction of the original draft of the second page of the Declaration.*

Compare the wording of the charges in Jefferson's draft of the Declaration with the wording of the preamble. The preamble form begins with Whereas George, *requiring that each charge start with the word* by. *The Declaration, presenting a list of facts to be submitted to a candid world (page 15, line 31), permits Jefferson to begin each charge with* he has, *repeatedly reminding readers of the villainous King. That Jefferson used the preamble as a basis for the charges in the Declaration can be seen not only from the order of the charges, but from the notes he wrote between the sixth and seventh charges of the preamble. These notes refer to three charges that were inserted into the Declaration at just that point (lines 19 through 24). In the Declaration, Jefferson omitted the second* m in accommodation *(line 6) and had his own way of spelling* unacknowledged *(line 28).* Prevent the population *(line 15) means* prevent the settlement. Raising the conditions of *(line 17) means* increasing the requirements for; *that is, making it more difficult to buy land.* Mean time *(line 13) today is written as one word to distinguish it from a special astronomical kind of time, as in* Greenwich mean time.

Whereas George   Guelph king of Great Britain and Ireland and Elector of Hanover, heretofore entrusted with the exercise of the kingly office in this government hath endeavored to pervert the same into a detestable and insupportable tyranny

1. by putting his negative on laws the most wholesome & necessary for ye. public good
   ~~had kept some colonies without judiciary establishments~~

2. by denying to his governors permission to pass laws of ~~the most~~ immediate & pressing im-
                      as
   -portance, unless suspended in their operation for his ~~consent~~, and when so suspended,
   neglecting ~~for nn~~ to attend to them for many years;

3. by refusing to pass certain other laws, unless the persons to be benefited by them would relinquish the inestimable rights of representation in the legislature;

4. by dissolving legislative assemblies repeatedly and continually for opposing with manly firm- -ness his invasions on the rights of the people;

5. when dissolved, by refusing to call others for a long space of time, thereby leaving the poli- -tical system [~~in a state of dissolution~~] without any legislative head;

                                       & for that purpose

6. by endeavouring to prevent the population of our country by obstructing the laws [for the
   encouraging the importation   *new*   *ons ~~new~~ of*
   naturalization] of foreigners & raising the conditions of appropriating lands;
   refused judiciary establmts . . .
   judges dependant
   erected swarms of offices

7. by keeping among us, in times of peace, standing armies & ships of war;

8. by affecting to render the military independent of & superior to the civil power;

                                             as

9. by combining with others to subject us to a foreign jurisdiction, giving his ~~consent~~ to their pretended acts of legislation ~~for imposing taxes on us without our consent~~

                              g
   a. for quartering large bodies of troops among us: & protect them &c—murders
   b. for cutting òff our trade with all parts of the world;
   c. for ~~depriving us~~ imposing taxes on us without our consent;
   d. for depriving us of the benefits of trial by jury;
   e. for transporting us beyond seas to be tried for pretended offences;
       for taking away our charters & altering fundamentally the forms of our government
   f. for suspending our own legislatures & declaring themselves invested with power
       to legislate for us in all cases whatsoever;

16.

10. by plundering our seas, ravaging our coasts, burning our towns and destroying the lives of our people;

14. 13.

                             citizens

11. by inciting insurrections of our fellow ~~subjects~~ with allurement of forfeiture & confiscation
                            by an inhuman use of his negative

12. by prompting our negroes to rise in arms among us; those very negroes whom he hath ~~from time to time~~ refused us permission to exclude by law:

13. by endeavoring to bring on the inhabitants of our frontiers the merciless Indian savages
                               of existence ~~*of life*~~
    whose known rule of warfare is undistinguished destruction of all ages, sexes & conditions

14. by transporting at this time a large army of foreign mercenaries to compleat the works of
                   with circumstances of cruelty & perfidy   *nation*
    death, desolation, & tyranny already begun in a stile so unworthy the head of a civilized ~~people~~
                for redress with a repetition of

15. by answering our repeated petitions ~~against this repeated~~ injuryies; ~~with a repetition of injuries~~

16. and finally by abandoning the helm of government & declaring us out of his allegiance & protection

Constitution of Virginia
First Ideas of Th: J
Communicated to a member of the Convention

1 he has refused his assent to laws the most wholesome and necessary for the pub-

2 -lic good:

3 he has forbidden his governors to pass laws of immediate & pressing importance,

4 unless suspended in their operation till his assent should be obtained;

5 and when so suspended, he has neglected utterly to attend to them.

6 he has refused to pass other laws for the accomodation of large districts of people

7 unless those people would relinquish the right of representation; a right

8 inestimable to them & formidable to tyrants alone:

9 he has dissolved Representative houses repeatedly & continually, for opposing with

10 manly firmness his invasions on the rights of the people;

11 he has refused for a long space of time to cause others to be elected,

12 whereby the legislative powers, incapable of annihilation, have returned to

13 the people at large for their exercise, the state remaining in the mean time

14 exposed to all the dangers of invasion from without & convulsions within:

15 he has endeavored to prevent the population of these states; for that purpose

16 obstructing the laws for naturalization of foreigners; refusing to pass others

17 to encourage their migrations hither; & raising the conditions of new ap-

18 -propriations of lands:

19 he has suffered the administration of justice totally to cease in some of these

20 colonies, refusing his assent to laws for establishing judiciary powers:

21 he has made our judges dependant on his will alone, for the tenure of their offices,

22 and amount of their salaries:

23 he has erected a multitude of new offices by a self-assumed power, & sent hi-

24 -ther swarms of officers to harrass our people & eat out their substance:

25 he has kept among us in times of peace standing armies & ships of war:

26 he has affected to render the military, independant of & superior to the civil power:

27 he has combined with others to subject us to a jurisdiction foreign to our constitu-

28 -tions and unacknoleged by our laws; giving his assent to their pretended acts

29 of legislation, for quartering large bodies of armed troops among us;

30 for protecting them by a mock-trial from punishment for any murders

31 they should commit on the inhabitants of these states;

32 for cutting off our trade with all parts of the world;

33 for imposing taxes on us without our consent;

34 for depriving us of the benefits of trial by jury;

35 for transporting us beyond seas to be tried for pretended offenses;

1   for taking away our charters, & altering fundamentally the forms of our governments;

2   for suspending our own legislatures & declaring themselves invested with power to

3   legislate for us in all cases whatsoever.

4 he has abdicated government here, withdrawing his governors, & declaring us out

5   of his allegiance & protection:

6 he has plundered our seas, ravaged our coasts, burnt our towns & destroyed the

7   lives of our people;

8 he is at this time transporting large armies of foreign mercenaries to compleat

9   the works of death, desolation & tyranny, already begun with circumstances

10   of cruelty & perfidy unworthy the head of a civilized nation:

11 he has endeavored to bring on the inhabitants of our frontiers the merciless Indian

12   savages, whose known rule of warfare is an undistinguished destruction of

13   all ages, sexes, & conditions of existence:

14 he has incited treasonable insurrections of our fellow-subjects, with the

15   allurements of forfeiture & confiscation of our property:

16 he has waged cruel war against human nature itself, violating it's most sa-

17   -cred rights of life & liberty in the persons of a distant people who never of-

18   -fended him, captivating & carrying them into slavery in another hemi-

19   -sphere, or to incur miserable death in their transportation thither. this

20   piratical warfare, the opprobrium of infidel powers, is the warfare of the

21   Christian king of Great Britain. determined to keep open a market

22   where MEN should be bought & sold, he has prostituted his negative

23   for suppressing every legislative attempt to prohibit or to restrain this

24   execrable commerce: and that this assemblage of horrors might want no fact

25   of distinguished die, he is now exciting those very people to rise in arms

26   among us, and to purchase that liberty of which he has deprived them,

27   by murdering the people upon whom he also obtruded them; thus paying

28   off former crimes committed against the liberties of one people, with crimes

29   which he urges them to commit against the lives of another.

30 in every stage of these oppressions we have petitioned for redress in the most humble

31 terms; our repeated petitions have been answered by repeated injury. a prince

32 whose character is thus marked by every act which may define a tyrant, is unfit

33 to be the ruler of a people who mean to be free. future ages will scarce believe

34 that the hardiness of one man, adventured within the short compass of 12 years

35 only, on so many acts of tyranny without a mask, over a people fostered & fixed in principles

36 of liberty.

Left: *Reconstruction of the third page of the original draft of the Declaration.*

The order of the last seven charges of the preamble has been rearranged. The twelfth charge in the preamble, now the next to last in the Declaration (line 16), has become the long new charge on slavery. The next-to-last charge in the preamble has been moved to the last position in the Declaration and has been extensively rewritten.

Captivating *(line 18) today means* enchanting. *Jefferson used it as a synonym for* capturing. *Today, someone writing the final sentence would use* ventured *in place of* adventured *(line 34).* Compleat *(line 8) was a common way of spelling* complete.

Below: *Reconstruction of part of the fourth page of the original draft of the Declaration.*

Jefferson's accusations against the British people deaf to the voice of justice *(line 12) would not, as we shall see, sit well with many of his fellow delegates in Congress. And when he asserted that the settlement of America was* unassisted by the wealth or the strength of Great Britain *(line 6), he was stretching facts to the breaking point. Just a dozen years before, Britain had made the colonies secure by driving the French from North America.*

1   Nor have we been wanting in attentions to our British brethren. we have

2   warned them from time to time of attempts by their legislature to extend a juris-

3   -diction over these our states. we have reminded them of the circumstances of

4   our emigration & settlement here, no one of which could warrant so strange a

5   pretension: that these were effected at the expence of our own blood & treasure,

6   unassisted by the wealth or the strength of Great Britain: that in constituting

7   indeed our several forms of government, we had adopted one common king, thereby

8   laying a foundation for perpetual league & amity with them: but that submission to their

9   parliament was no part of our constitution, nor ever in idea, if history may be

10   credited: and we appealed to their native justice & magnanimity, as well as to the ties

11   of our common kindred to disavow these usurpations which were likely to interrupt

12   our correspondence & connection. they too have been deaf to the voice of justice &

13   of consanguinity, & when occasions have been given them, by the regular course of

14   their laws, of removing from their councils the disturbers of our harmony, they

15   have by their free election re-established them in power.

Now, more satisfied with the charges, Jefferson was ready to pick up where he had left off the previous morning.

very too they
~~and~~ at this time are permitting their ~~sovereign~~ chief magistrate to
only   common   invade and
send over not soldiers of our ~~own~~ blood but foreign mercenaries to ~~destroy~~

He made one change.

only   common   Scotch &   invade and
send over not soldiers of our ~~own~~ blood but foreign mercenaries to ~~destroy~~

We can assume this change was not made before June 19, because Congress had only received word of the capture of one hundred Scottish Highlanders at sea on the morning of June 18, in a letter forwarded by General Washington.

The desk at which Jefferson wrote the Declaration. It was made to Jefferson's design by Benjamin Randolph, the Philadelphia cabinetmaker at whose home Jefferson resided in 1775 and in 1776 before moving to the Graff house. The 1¾" deep drawer is divided into sections for holding paper and pens, and has a compartment for a small glass inkwell. While writing, Jefferson kept the drawer open to get at the ink. The writing surface unfolded to an area 14⅜" wide and 19¾" long. It was lined with green baize, the softness of which was no detriment to writing on the heavy paper then in use. Jefferson gave the desk to his granddaughter, Ellen Randolph (no relation to Benjamin the cabinetmaker), when she married Joseph Coolidge in Boston, in 1825. (Smithsonian Institution, Washington, D.C.)

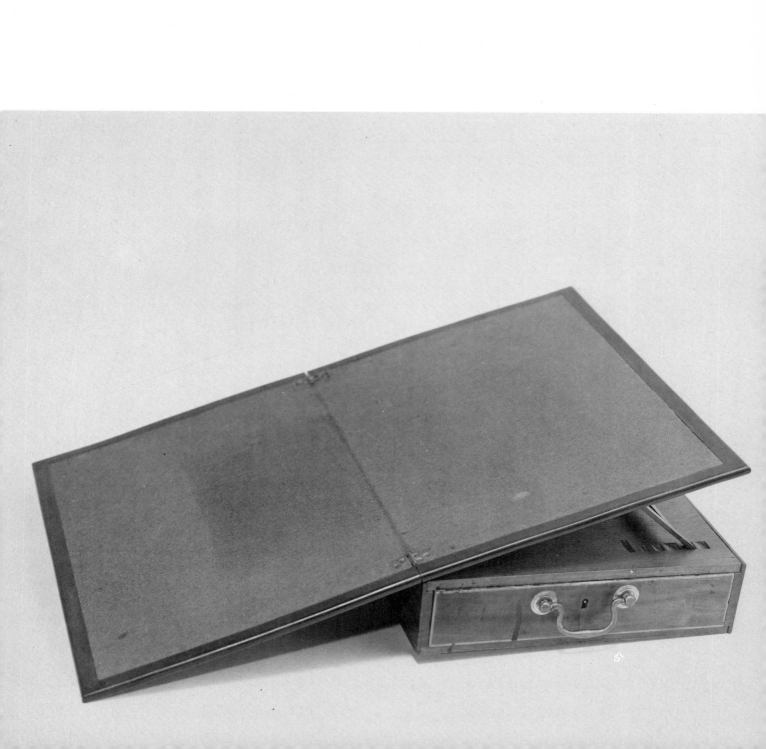

1   *very*   *too they*
1 ~~this conduct and~~ at this∧time∧are permitting their ~~sovereign~~ chief magistrate to

2   *only*   *common*   *Scotch &*   *invade and*
2 send over not∧soldiers of our ~~own~~∧blood but∧foreign mercenaries to ~~destroy~~

3 *deluge us in blood. these facts have given the last stab to agonizing affection, & manly spirit bids us to*
3 ~~us. this is too much to be borne even by relations. enough be it to say we are~~

4 *renounce for ever these unfeeling brethren.*
4 ~~now done with them!~~ we must endeavor to forget our former love for them

5   *we hold*
5 and to hold them, as∧the rest of mankind, enemies in war, in peace friends.

6   *free*   *great*   *a*   *grandeur*
6 we might have been a ~~great~~ & a ~~happy~~ people together, but∧communicat~~ed~~ion of ~~happiness~~

7   *freedom*   *low*
7 & of ~~grandeur~~ it seems is be~~neath~~ their dignity. ~~we will climb then the roads to glory &~~

8   *& to glory*
8 ~~happiness apart~~ be it so, since they will have it: the road to ~~glory & to~~ happiness∧

9   *apart from them*
9 is open to us too, we will climb it ~~in a separate state,~~ & acquiesce in the necessity

10   *de*
10 which ~~pro~~nounces our ~~everlasting Adieu.~~ eternal separation.

11 ~~these facts have given the last stab to agonizing affection, & manly spirit bids~~

12   *unfeeling*
12 ~~us to renounce for ever these unjust brethren.~~

Left: *Jefferson's work sheet for part of the paragraph at the top of the fourth page of the Declaration, found in the Library of Congress in 1947 by Professor Julian Boyd.* (Library of Congress)

This work sheet is part of one of the pages Jefferson made by folding an 11″ × 14″ sheet in half. The top is torn off, leaving only part of a sentence, re-establish them in power, *which is not visible here. At the bottom of the sheet (and upside down) is part of a resolution on General Sullivan that Jefferson wrote several weeks later.*

Above: *Reconstruction of Jefferson's work sheet.*

Notice (lines 11 and 12) that Jefferson composed a new sentence in the empty space below, before inserting it above lines 3 and 4. The substitution of invade and deluge us in blood *for* destroy us *(lines 2 and 3) is an example of the florid style that Jefferson avoided in most parts of the Declaration. When he becomes emotional, as in this passage, his style deteriorates. He is at his best in making plain statements that express ideas.*

The changes at the end of line 8 and on lines 9 and 10 were made later, but before Jefferson showed the original draft to Adams. For some reason, Jefferson went back and inserted them in the work sheet.

Having finished the next-to-the-last paragraph, Jefferson was now ready to tackle the last, with its announcement of independence. He reread Richard Henry Lee's resolution:

> That these United Colonies are, and of right ought to be,
> free and independent States, that they are absolved from
> all allegiance to the British Crown, and that all political
> connection between them and the State of Great Britain
> is, and ought to be, totally dissolved . . .

Jefferson decided to change the wording, to make it more legal. He would get to that later. He put it aside and passed his eyes over the last words of the previous morning's work:

> ~~happiness apart~~ *be it so, since they will have it. the road to glory & to happiness*
> *is open to us too, we will climb it in a separate state, & acquiesce in the necessity*
> *which pronounces our everlasting Adieu.*

and was ready to begin. He took a scrap of paper on which he had started a letter, turned it over, and labored over the last paragraph, scratching through words and writing others, adding changes between the lines. It was almost half past six when he was satisfied. A mosquito whined around his head. It landed on his ear and he slapped it. Bob Hemings woke with a start, scrambled to his feet, pulled on his shoes, and went downstairs to heat the tea water.

Jefferson took a new sheet of paper and folded it in half. He was now ready to put the two parts of the Declaration together. From the first page of the old folder he copied onto the first page of the new folder, the first two paragraphs of the Declaration. On the second and third (inside) pages went the list of charges. They ended about two-thirds of the way down the third page, which left room for a paragraph summarizing how the colonists felt about the King's acts and the King himself. This summary Jefferson transferred from the second page of the old folder.

On the fourth page of the new folder went the paragraph that covered the top half of the third page of the old folder, the paragraph about Scotch and foreign mercenaries, on which he had spent so much time. It was followed by the final paragraph, announcing independence.

Right: *Reconstruction of the fourth page of the original draft of the Declaration.*

Jefferson's announcement of independence (lines 26 to 37) is now longer and more legal-sounding than the Richard Henry Lee resolution. Lee's absolve all allegiance became reject and renounce all allegiance & subjection (line 28). To Lee's reference to the British Crown Jefferson added & all others who may hereafter claim by, through, or under them (line 29).

1   Nor have we been wanting in attentions to our British brethren. we have
2   warned them from time to time of attempts by their legislature to extend a juris-
3   -diction over these our states. we have reminded them of the circumstances of
4   our emigration & settlement here, no one of which could warrant so strange a
5   pretension: that these were effected at the expence of our own blood & treasure,
6   unassisted by the wealth or the strength of Great Britain: that in constituting
7   indeed our several forms of government, we had adopted one common king, thereby
8   laying a foundation for perpetual league & amity with them: but that submission to their
9   parliament was no part of our constitution, nor ever in idea, if history may be
10   credited: and we appealed to their native justice & magnanimity, as well as to the ties
11   of our common kindred to disavow these usurpations which were likely to interrupt
12   our correspondence & connection. they too have been deaf to the voice of justice &
13   of consanguinity, & when occasions have been given them, by the regular course of
14   their laws, of removing from their councils the disturbers of our harmony, they
15   have by their free election re-established them in power. at this very time too they
16   are permitting their chief magistrate to send over not only soldiers of our common
17   blood, but Scotch & foreign mercenaries to invade & deluge us in blood. these facts
18   have given the last stab to agonizing affection and manly spirit bids us to re-
19   -nounce for ever these unfeeling brethren. we must endeavor to forget our former
20   love for them, and to hold them as we hold the rest of mankind, enemies in war,
21   in peace friends. we might have been a free & a great people together; but a commu-
22   -nication of grandeur & of freedom it seems is below their dignity. be it so, since they
23   will have it; the road to glory & happiness is open to us too; we will climb it in
24   a separate state, and acquiesce in the necessity which pronounces our ever-
25   -lasting Adieu!

26   We therefore the representatives of the United States of America in General Con-
27   -gress assembled do, in the name & by authority of the good people of these states,
28   reject and renounce all allegiance & subjection to the kings of Great Britain
29   & all others who may hereafter claim by, through, or under them; we utterly
30   dissolve & break off all political connections which may have heretofore sub-
31   -sisted between us & the people or parliament of Great Britain; and finally
32   we do assert and declare these colonies to be free and independant states,
33   and that as free & independant states they shall hereafter have power to levy
34   war, conclude peace, contract alliances, establish commerce, & to do all other
35   acts and things which independant states may of right do. for the
36   support of this declaration we mutually pledge to each other our lives, our
37   fortunes, & our sacred honour.

It was almost eight o'clock when he finished copying. The city was stirring. The document was completed.

Jefferson had written the Declaration, particularly the first and fourth pages and the long slavery charge, with great care. Writing is not a science, to be reduced like mathematics to rules. Even if the meaning of a word is precise, it is colored by its surroundings. The writer selects words by intuition, for reasons he cannot always explain. The deeper their source, the greater his attachment to them.

He suffers when others alter or rearrange them. Jefferson would now have to submit his words to the committee.

CHAPTER SEVEN

An Earlier Declaration—1775

Jefferson had already had unpleasant experiences writing for Congress. He had been given many writing assignments when he first came to Philadelphia in June 1775, because he was known as the author of *A Summary View of the Rights of British America*, published in Williamsburg, Virginia, and London in 1774.

No one had changed a word of *A Summary View*. Jefferson had written it as a set of instructions to Virginia's delegates to the First Continental Congress in 1774, and sent it to some friends. They had liked it so much that they had paid to have it printed. And none of those who had read the printed version had told him that anything was wrong with it. When he wrote a report for Congress, however, Jefferson found that any part of his work could be questioned. He had never gotten over his first experience in writing a declaration for Congress.

Almost as soon as he had arrived in Philadelphia in 1775, he had been added to a committee that had been formed to write a Declaration on the Causes and Necessity of Taking Up Arms. The committee needed a writer because a draft of the declaration by John Rutledge (Edward's older brother) had been found unacceptable and had been rejected.

At that time, June 1775, just two months after armed resistance to Britain had begun at Lexington and Concord, there were two factions in Congress: a minority who could see no further hope of reconciliation, and a majority who thought that there was still a chance for a peaceful solution that would leave the colonies in the empire.

The Declaration of Causes could also be called a "declaration of dependence," since it was intended to reassure the British that Americans had no desire for separation but were only asking for justice. It was to be accompanied by the Olive Branch Petition to the King (see Chapter 2), holding out the hand of peace.

John Dickinson, leader of the reconciliation-seeking majority, was a tall and slender man of forty-four who was as tough as steel cable. His father had sent him to England for his legal education. He had spent three years in London, at the Middle Temple. Like many other members of Congress who had studied or worked in London, he had a great attachment to the beauties and refinements of life in that metropolis. Except for Benjamin Franklin, no man in Congress at that time had more of a reputation than Dickinson as a writer. Dickinson's fame as an author had resulted from his *Letters of a Pennsylvania Farmer*, published in 1767-68. These stated that Parliament had a right to regulate the colonies' trade, but not to levy taxes that would only fatten the imperial treasury.

Dickinson had been added to the declaration committee along with Jefferson. Since, however, he was already writing the Olive Branch Petition, it was left to Jefferson to replace John Rutledge's draft of the declaration with a better one.

Jefferson and Dickinson barely knew one another when the Virginian showed his draft to his fellow penman. Reading it over, Dickinson saw that the four-page paper had many of the same features that had made Rutledge's draft objectionable. Southerners loved the sound and flow of words and preferred high-sounding generalities to facts. But Dickinson, careful of hurting the newcomer's feelings, trod lightly on Jefferson's prose.

He suggested only eleven changes in wording. Eight of these came in the list of charges. Jefferson had begun the first:

> her parliament then for the first time
> asserted a right of unbounded legislation
> over the colonies of America.

Dickinson suggested:

> *by their influence*
> ∧her parliament then for the first time
> *were persuaded to assume and assert*
> ~~asserted~~ a right of unbounded legislation
> over the colonies of America.

Further on, Jefferson had written:

> they have declared that American subjects
> charged with certain offenses shall be
> transported beyond sea to be tried before the
> very persons against whose pretended
> sovereignty offense is supposed to be committed;

Dickinson suggested that the last line be changed:

> _the_
> sovereignty ᴧ offense is supposed to be committed;

Jefferson had written:

> & laying waste property until suppressed
> by the people suddenly assembled . . .

Dickinson suggested:

> & laying waste property until suppressed
> _Country who_
> by the ᴧ people ᴧ suddenly assembled . . .

And Jefferson had written:

> the inhabitants of the town of Boston having
> entered into treaty with a certain Thomas Gage
> principal instigator of the enormities, it was
> stipulated that the said inhabitants having first . . .

Dickinson suggested:

> the inhabitants of the town of Boston having
> _General Gage_
> entered into treaty with ~~a certain Thomas Gage~~
> _to procure their enlargement_
> ~~principal instigator of the enormities,~~ it was
> _after_
> stipulated that the said inhabitants ᴧ having first . . .

Dickinson's three other suggestions for changes in wording came on the last page of the Declaration of Causes, where Jefferson reassured the readers that independence was _not_ the aim of the colonists:

> But that this declaration may not disquiet
> the minds of our fellow subjects in any
> part of the empire . . .

Dickinson made the following changes:

But that this declaration may not disquiet

friends &   *in Britain or other*

the minds of our ‸ fellow subjects ~~in any~~

s

part ‸ of the empire . . .

Dickinson also suggested four pieces of additional information to add facts in support of Jefferson's arguments.

Eleven small changes must be considered light and respectful editing of a document that runs to two thousand words. Nor should the four suggested additions, which Jefferson could have put in his own words, have presented any great difficulty.

Jefferson rejected all four of the additions and seven of the eleven changes in wording. The only wording changes he accepted were the added *the* in

the

(1) *whose pretended sovereignty* ‸ *offense is supposed to be committed;*

(2) the substitution of *General Gage* for *a certain Thomas Gage;*

(3) the phrase *to procure their enlargement* (meaning to procure their freedom), which he changed slightly to *in order to procure their enlargement.* (In accepting this, he accepted the deletion of *principal instigator of the enormities.*)

(4) the addition of *friends &* in the sentence *But that this declaration may not disquiet the minds of our friends & fellow subjects. . . .*

Changes in wording almost always alter meaning in some degree. It is this aspect of editing that is of most concern to writers, who spend considerable time searching for the most exact way of conveying what they want to say. Dickinson's first recommendations went the furthest in changing Jefferson's meaning, for in qualifying

> her parliament then for the first time
> assumed a power of unbounded legislation
> over the colonies

with

> *by their influence*
> ‸ her parliament then for the first time
> *were persuaded to assume and assert*
> ~~asserted~~ a right of unbounded legislation
> over the colonies

Dickinson was pushing the blame away from Parliament who, he was saying, was under the *influence* of the King's ministers, who *persuaded* it to *assume* and *assert.*

Jefferson changed *asserted a right* to *assumed a power*, borrowing a word from Dickinson, but resented the attempt to change what he wanted to say.

It was not clear why he rejected the other five wording changes, all of which made the sentences clearer. His rejection of most of what could only be considered very light editing of his Declaration of Causes shows that he was extremely sensitive to criticism.

Later Jefferson showed the almost unchanged draft to the rest of the committee. They did not like it, and it was taken out of Jefferson's hands. One member, William Livingston of New Jersey (an older cousin of Robert Livingston's), found it no better than the rejected draft of John Rutledge. He wrote a friend that

> Both had the faults common to our Southern gentlemen. Much fault-finding and declamation, with little sense of dignity. They seem to think a reiteration of tyranny, despotism, bloody, &c. all that is needed to unite us at home . . .

The dispute in the committee seems to have been bitter, since work on the Declaration of Causes was halted until the deadline was missed. General Washington was to have read the declaration to his troops when he joined them at Cambridge, Massachusetts, on July 6, 1775. To reach the general on that date, the declaration would have had to have left Philadelphia no later than July 2, 1775. But on July 2, the committee still had not agreed on a text. The writing of the Declaration of Causes was probably taken out of Jefferson's hands more because of his unwillingness to accept suggestions than because it was unsuitable. When Dickinson finally rewrote it he followed Jefferson's basic form and used a lot of Jefferson's language. Dickinson's version was a page longer, but about half the words were still Jefferson's.

In neither version was this declaration an inspired document. But there were some places where Dickinson had definitely improved it.

In describing how the British governor of Massachusetts, General Gage, had broken a treaty with the people of Charlestown, detaining them after promising them freedom, and compelling "those permitted to depart . . . to leave their most valuable effects behind. . . ," Jefferson had written:

> we leave the world it's own reflection on this atrocious perfidy.

Dickinson put it this way:

> By this perfidy Wives are separated from their Husbands, Children from their Parents, the aged and the sick from

43

their Relations and Friends, who wish to attend and comfort them; and those who have been used to live in Plenty and even Elegance, are reduced to deplorable Distress.

And compare these sentences near the end of Jefferson's draft with the final version:

Jefferson

But that this declaration may not disquiet the minds of our Friends & fellow subjects in any part of the empire, we do further assure them that we mean not in any wise to affect that union with them in which we have so long & happily lived, and which we wish so much to see again restored. that necessity must be hard indeed which may force upon us to avail ourselves of any aid which their enemies might proffer. we did not embody a soldiery to commit aggression on them . . .

Dickinson

Lest this Declaration should disquiet the Minds of our Friends and Fellow-Subjects in any part of the Empire, we assure them that we mean not to dissolve the Union which has so long and so happily subsisted between us, and which we sincerely wish to see restored. Necessity has not yet driven us into that desperate Measure, or induced us to excite any other Nation to War against them. We have not raised Armies with ambitious Designs of separating from Great-Britain, and establishing Independent States.

Dickinson's changes did not appear as improvements to Jefferson, who felt that his words, thoughts, and feelings had been corrupted.

Now, in June 1776, Jefferson was about to submit a draft of another declaration—on independence—to another committee. If the other four members—John Adams, Benjamin Franklin, Robert Livingston, and Roger Sherman—disputed his words, he might abandon this Declaration, too, to the pen of another.

John Adams would be the first to see it.

CHAPTER EIGHT

John Adams, Editor

Our clue concerning the Scotch "mercenaries" gives us Wednesday, June 19, 1776, as the earliest date for completion of the original draft of the Declaration. For other reasons, as we shall see, we must assume that it was either on that very morning, or the next, that Jefferson showed the Rough Draft (copied from the original draft, and with 12 changes) to John Adams.

To get to Adams's residence, Jefferson and Bob Hemings headed east toward the Schuylkill River. It was a cloudy morning, and a damp wind came up from the water.

If it was Wednesday, the 19th, it was market day, and wooden carts laden with sides of beef, barrels of salt pork, live chickens, fresh muttons, flour, and cider rumbled down High Street toward the arcades. Jefferson always liked to visit the markets, to see what vegetables and fruits were in season and to compare their sizes and forms with those he grew in Virginia. At Fourth Street, when he reached the market, he got down from his horse, tied it to a post, and strolled through the covered passage. He liked the thick odor of earth and freshly picked greens, and enjoyed watching housewives in their bonnets haggling over the prices of onions and eggs, and criticizing the way the butchers cut their meat.

He rode past the courthouse, built over other market arcades, and turned north to Arch Street, where John Adams was staying.

The New Englanders were a different breed. Jefferson was intrigued by the way John Adams lived in a boardinghouse down by the waterfront, without any servants. Jefferson supposed that all this—the rumble of hogsheads over planks, the damp tar smell of rigging—seemed like home to his colleague from Boston.

What would Adams do? The Declaration was not supposed to be anything original. Everyone knew the arguments for independence. Adams had stated them a hundred times, but not *quite* as they appeared on the first page of Jefferson's

45

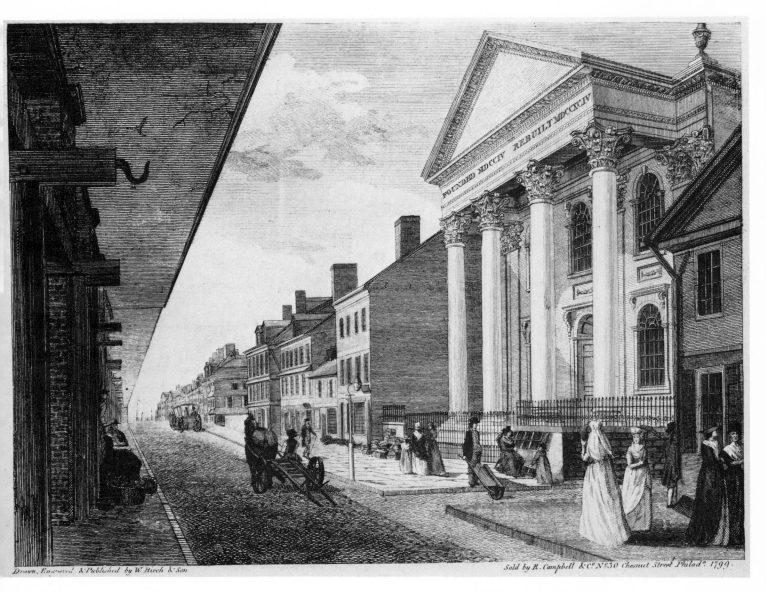

High Street in Philadelphia (now called Market Street), looking east toward the Delaware River. The market stalls that would give the street its name are seen to the left. The Graff house, where Jefferson stayed, is several blocks to the west. (If you were standing where the artist stood when he made this picture, looking east toward the river, the Graff house would be in back of you, several blocks away.) This engraving was made in 1799, but except for the clothing styles, the scene is close to what Jefferson would have observed riding down to the wharves to cast an eye over ship arrivals. (Library of Congress)

draft. Jefferson had encased a sunbeam in a frame of words, creating a fragile construction that a critic might shatter without knowing.

Having just put on his vest to greet his visitor, Adams was alert with the look of a man who had been at work for hours. He was brisk yet pleasant, clutching Jefferson's papers in his firm right hand and promising a quick opinion. Jefferson rode away to attend yet another committee meeting, and Adams returned to his rooms.

John Adams was very different from Jefferson. Jefferson was tall and slender, his bearing loose and languid. Adams was a head shorter and quick in motion. Jefferson always was well disciplined, with a system for everything. Adams never had enough time to finish anything to his satisfaction. Jefferson sat quietly in Congress, rarely offering an opinion. Adams was usually in the thick of debate.

Jefferson was one of the biggest landholders in Virginia and an aristocrat. Adams was the son of a plain Massachusetts farmer and made his living in the law courts. Jefferson, who had grown up on the Virginia frontier, who had never seen twenty houses together until he was eighteen, who ruled a feudal barony in which almost all the hard labor was done by slaves, trusted "the people." Adams, coming from the great town of Boston and having experienced city mobs, distrusted "the people."

At the same time that he was zealous for independence, Adams was aware that the colonists were turning themselves loose from everything that had brought peace, regularity, and order to their lives—that had protected men from the beasts within their breasts. He kept thinking of a former client who was pleased that the revolution had stopped the Massachusetts courts:

> Oh! Mr. Adams what great Things you and your Colleagues have done for Us! . . . There are no Courts of Justice now in this Province, and I hope there never will be another!

In disgust, Adams had wondered if he had been working so hard and taking such risks to allow ne'er-do-wells to escape paying their debts.

Since the dawn of history, men had believed themselves to be creatures of the state, their duties defined by law and custom. The new natural law philosophy put man before the state. It said that the state was made for the individual, that a government was worthwhile only as long as it served the people's needs. Under the old rules, people served the state. Under natural law, the state served the people.

If men set up governments and laws, who was to say that the men who did so were themselves lawful? And if they were not lawful, what did that make of their governments? Many colonists looked upon the rebels' new provincial assemblies as

John Adams, as seen by his fellow Bostonian, John Singleton Copley, in London, in the fall of 1783. Copley, a Loyalist, had left their native city in 1774. Adams, who had just negotiated the treaty with England that settled the war, is shown with a statue of Peace in the background, pointing to a map of the new United States of America. He paid Copley 100 guineas for this life-size work. (Harvard University Portrait Collection, Bequest of Ward Nicholas Boylston in 1828)

self-appointed groups of ruffians who had seized by force what they could not get by the old laws rooted in English tradition.

If men made one law or government today, could they not make another tomorrow? Could they not change everything to suit their immediate wishes? What was to make rebels, who now found themselves as the source of law, obey anything that they did not like?

The governments of Europe solved this problem by tracing their authority back to an outside and superior source (our Lord GEORGE the third, by the Grace of *God*, of Great Britain . . . King).

What American would see divine authority in an assembly of his equals or in a Continental Congress?

Where Adams saw dangers, Jefferson saw opportunities. Seeing less virtue in established governments than Adams, Jefferson believed that ordinary men could not rule themselves worse than they had been governed by Old World despots. The minds of Adams and Jefferson met on some points—on the need for independence—and departed on others.

Adams chewed tobacco, a habit considered coarse by some of the finer gentlemen in Congress. He was vain and full of self-doubt and envy. The year before, after having ridden out of Philadelphia with other members of Congress as escort to generals Washington, Charles Lee, and Philip Schuyler, he had written his wife, Abigail:

> I, poor creature, worn out with scribbling for my bread
> and my liberty, low in spirits and weak in health, must
> leave others to wear the laurels which I have sewn; others
> to eat the bread which I have earned . . .

Adams knew as well as anyone the difficulty of writing for Congress. Most of his first six weeks in Philadelphia, at the First Continental Congress in the fall of 1774, had been spent in a committee struggling over a Declaration of Rights. The members of the committee had two main areas of disagreement: (1) whether to base the rights of the colonies on natural law or on the British constitution, and (2) how much authority to concede Parliament.

The first argument was settled by stating that the colonies had both natural rights and rights gained from the evolution of British Law. But the second question, on Parliament's authority, could not be resolved. With the entire Declaration of Rights written except for the part dealing with the foremost issue, the task seemed hopeless. As a last resort, South Carolina's John Rutledge turned to Adams:

Adams We must agree upon Something: you appear as familiar with the Subject as any of Us, and I like your Expressions *the necessity of the Case* and *excluding all ideas of taxation external and internal.* . . . Come take the Pen and see if you cant produce something that will unite Us.

John Adams took a sheet of paper and drew up an article which—while it satisfied no one—was recognized as the best that all could agree on. His statement said less than he and Sam Adams wanted, but more than those seeking reconciliation had been prepared to say.

Adams had had his fill of writing for Congress, as well as hearing the addresses, petitions, and declarations of others. He could see no benefit worth the efforts they had expended in 1774 over the Declaration of Rights or in 1775 over the Declaration of Causes. The Olive Branch Petition, he believed, had actually worked mischief by arousing false hopes—beguiling the colonies into believing that they would accomplish with pen and ink what could only be won by resistance. Such a man was John Adams, who now had the four pages of Jefferson's draft of the Declaration of Independence in his hand.

CHAPTER NINE

A Problem of Prisoners

On Thursday, June 20, 1776, Congress spent a good part of the day discussing a report Jefferson had written about an agreement that General Benedict Arnold had made in Canada with Captain Forster of the British army.

The ugly business had occurred in May at the Cedars, an American fortification forty-three miles above Montreal on the south side of the St. Lawrence River. It was a case of one man's failing putting others in difficulty. Major Butterfield of the American army had surrendered his garrison of 390 men without a fight, while reinforcements from nearby were on the way. Because of Butterfield's surrender, his British captor, Captain Forster, had been able to also capture Major Sherburne and 120 reinforcements in spite of their stiff resistance.

When the American General Benedict Arnold arrived a few days later with a large force, Captain Forster threatened to kill all 500 American prisoners in his hands. Instead of driving the British from the Cedars, Arnold was forced to negotiate. Under the agreement of May 27, 1776, known as the Cedars Cartel, the American prisoners were handed over to Arnold, in exchange for future delivery of an equal number of British prisoners. As a guarantee of good faith, four hostages—captains in service under Arnold—were handed over to Forster.

Congress had to decide what to do about this agreement. A four-man committee chaired by Jefferson had taken testimony from Major Sherburne and submitted recommendations to Congress. The committee declared that Arnold had not been authorized to make an agreement concerning British prisoners who had been captured earlier and were not in his own custody, but in the hands of Congress. Thus Congress was not bound by the cartel, and could alter it. For one thing, the committee did not think that British prisoners ought to be exchanged for those Americans who had surrendered without a fight. It recommended that exchanges be made for Sherburne and his men, but that Major Butterfield and his men be returned to the British.

Jefferson's report was very controversial. The cartel had, in effect, passed on to Congress the pain with which General Arnold had been confronted. No course seemed satisfactory. Two of the captains in Butterfield's command, Stevens and Easterbrook, had wanted to fight; yet Jefferson and the committee would return them to the British, in effect punishing the officers for obeying the orders of their superior. Four of Arnold's captains had bravely given themselves up to the British as guarantors of the cartel. What would happen to them if Congress did not honor the terms of the agreement?

It was a long and wearing argument, Jefferson taking notes to be used in revising the report.

Assuming that Jefferson delivered the Rough Draft of the Declaration to Adams on the morning of the 19th, we have allowed him until the afternoon of the 20th to have made a copy for his own use and returned it to Jefferson.

Adams, like Dickinson a year earlier, was being careful of Jefferson's feelings. He disagreed with Jefferson's portrayal of King George as a tyrant on the bottom of the third page. Adams thought the attack too personal, "too passionate . . . too much like scolding for so grave and solemn a document." But he made no such comment when he handed the Declaration back to its author. He hoped that another committee member, perhaps Franklin or Sherman, would make that criticism.

Two or three changes and one suggested addition were not hard for the author to take. It was with a greater degree of confidence that Jefferson prepared to show the Declaration to the other members of the committee.

Right: *Reconstruction of the first page of the Declaration with additional changes made by Jefferson up to the time John Adams saw it, and including Adams's changes (circled).*

By the time he showed the Declaration to Adams, Jefferson had made twelve additional changes in its text, three on this page (lines 7, 22 and 23). Assuming that Adams changed the first of *in the title to* by, *he made two changes on this page. Perhaps in substituting* the King of Great Britain *for* his majesty *(line 27), Adams was trying to sound less like a subject and more like a citizen of a new, independent nation.*

A Declaration (by) ~~of~~ the Representatives of the
UNITED STATES OF AMERICA, *in General Congress assembled.*

1   When in the course of human events it becomes necessary for a people to

2   advance from that subordination in which they have hitherto remained, & to as-

3   -sume among the powers of the earth the equal & independant station to

4   which the laws of nature & of nature's god entitle them, a decent respect

5   to the opinions of mankind requires that they should declare the causes

6   which impel them to the change.

                self evident

7   We hold these truths to be ~~sacred & undeniable,~~ that all men are

8   created equal & independant, that from that equal creation they derive

9   rights inherent & inalienable, among which are the preservation of

10 life, & liberty & the pursuit of happiness; that to secure these ends, go-

11 -vernments are instituted among men, deriving their just powers from

12 the consent of the governed; that whenever any form of government

13 shall become destructive of these ends, it is the right of the people to alter

14 or to abolish it, & to institute new government, laying it's foundation on

15 such principles & organising it's powers in such form, as to them shall

16 seem most likely to effect their safety & happiness. prudence indeed

17 will dictate that governments long established should not be changed for

18 light & transient causes: and accordingly all experience hath shewn that

19 mankind are more disposed to suffer while evils are sufferable, than to

20 right themselves by abolishing the forms to which they are accustomed. but

21 when a long train of abuses & usurpations, begun at a distinguished period,

22 & pursuing invariably the same object, evinces a design to ~~subject~~ reduce

     under absolute

23 them ~~to arbitrary~~ power, it is their right, it is their duty, to throw off such

24 government & to provide new guards for their future security. such has

25 been the patient sufferance of these colonies; & such is now the necessity

26 which constrains them to expunge their former systems of government.

    (the) (King of Great Britain)

27 the history of ~~his~~ present ~~majesty,~~ is a history of unremitting injuries and

28 usurpations, among which no one fact stands single or solitary to contra-

29 -dict the uniform tenor of the rest, all of which have in direct object the

30 establishment of an absolute tyranny over these states. to prove this, let facts be

31 submitted to a candid world, for the truth of which we pledge a faith

32 yet unsullied by falsehood.

Right: *Reconstruction of the second page of the Declaration as John Adams saw it, and with his changes circled.*

John Adams made two changes on this page and may have suggested an additional charge against the King (see page 83). The change on line 11 clarified the charge by connecting it with the preceding charge (line 9). The change on line 20, from colonies *to* states, *was a reminder of the new status of America. Jefferson's substitution of* only *for* alone *(line 8), shown here as an interlineation, was actually made by writing one word on top of the other (see Rough Draft, page 82).*

Adams left the last two pages of the Declaration alone, although he had reservations about parts of them.

1 he has refused his assent to laws the most wholesome and necessary for the pub-

2 -lic good:

3 he has forbidden his governors to pass laws of immediate & pressing importance,

4   unless suspended in their operation till his assent should be obtained;

5   and when so suspended, he has neglected utterly to attend to them.

6 he has refused to pass other laws for the accomodation of large districts of people

7   unless those people would relinquish the right of representation; *in the legislature* a right

8   inestimable to them & formidable to tyrants *only* ~~alone:~~

9 he has dissolved Representative houses repeatedly & continually, for opposing with

10   manly firmness his invasions on the rights of the people:

11 he has refused for a long space of time (*after such Dissolutions*) to cause others to be elected,

12   whereby the legislative powers, incapable of annihilation, have returned to

13   the people at large for their exercise, the state remaining in the mean time

14   exposed to all the dangers of invasion from without & convulsions within;

15 he has endeavored to prevent the population of these states; for that purpose

16   obstructing the laws for naturalization of foreigners; refusing to pass others

17   to encourage their migrations hither; & raising the conditions of new ap-

18   -propriations of lands:

19 he has suffered the administration of justice totally to cease in some of these

20 ~~colonies,~~ (*states*) refusing his assent to laws for establishing judiciary powers:

21 he has made our judges dependant on his will alone, for the tenure of their offices,

22   and amount of their salaries:

23 he has erected a multitude of new offices by a self-assumed power, & sent hi-

24   -ther swarms of officers to harrass our people & eat out their substance:

25 he has kept among us in times of peace standing armies & ships of war:

26 he has affected to render the military, independant of & superior to the civil power:

27 he has combined with others to subject us to a jurisdiction foreign to our constitu-

28   -tions and unacknoleged by our laws; giving his assent to their pretended acts

29   of legislation, for quartering large bodies of armed troops among us;

30   for protecting them by a mock-trial from punishment for any murders

31   they should commit on the inhabitants of these states;

32   for cutting off our trade with all parts of the world;

33   for imposing taxes on us without our consent;

34   for depriving us of the benefits of trial by jury;

35   for transporting us beyond seas to be tried for pretended offences:

Right: *Reconstruction of the third page of the Declaration as John Adams saw it.*

The three alterations on this page were all made by Jefferson before he showed it to Adams. If Americans were severing themselves from King George, it made more sense to refer to them as citizens *(line 14) than as* subjects. *The entire slavery charge (lines 16 to 29) is a good example of the way Jefferson's lucid style tended to make even the most painful subject seem cool and manageable. Notice that at this time Jefferson was thinking of moving the clause* determined to keep open a market where MEN should be bought & sold *from lines 21 and 22 to follow the word* commerce *(line 24). When Adams made his copy of the Declaration, he started to put the clause after* Great Britain *(line 21) and then, crossing out the words* determined to, *he put the clause after* commerce *(line 24). Later (page 86), Jefferson, following his first inclination, decided to leave the clause on lines 21 and 22.*

1 for taking away our charters, & altering fundamentally the forms of our **governments**;

2 for suspending our own legislatures & declaring themselves invested with power to

3   legislate for us in all cases whatsoever.

4 he has abdicated government here, withdrawing his governors, & declaring us out

5   of his allegiance & protection:

6 he has plundered our seas, ravaged our coasts, burnt our towns & destroyed the

7   lives of our people;

8 he is at this time transporting large armies of foreign mercenaries to compleat

9   the works of death, desolation & tyranny, already begun with circumstances

10   of cruelty & perfidy unworthy the head of a civilized nation:

11 he has endeavored to bring on the inhabitants of our frontiers the merciless Indian

12   savages, whose known rule of warfare is an undistinguished destruction of

13   all ages, sexes, & conditions of existence:

14 he has incited treasonable insurrections of our fellow-~~subjects,~~ *citizens* with the

15   allurements of forfeiture & confiscation of our property:

16 he has waged cruel war against human nature itself, violating it's most sa-

17   -cred rights of life & liberty in the persons of distant people who never of-

18   -fended him, captivating & carrying them into slavery in another hemi-

19   -sphere, or to incur miserable death in their transportation thither. this

20   piratical warfare, the opprobrium of infidel powers, is the warfare of the

21   Christian king of Great Britain. [determined to keep open a market

22   where MEN should be bought & sold,] he has prostituted his negative

23   for suppressing every legislative attempt to prohibit or to restrain this

24   *determining to keep open a market where MEN should be bought & sold* execrable commerce: and that this assemblage of horrors might want no fact

25   of distinguished die, he is now exciting those very people to rise in arms

26   among us, and to purchase that liberty of which he has deprived them,

27   by murdering the people upon whom he also obtruded them; thus paying

28   off former crimes committed against the liberties of one people, with crimes

29   which he urges them to commit against the lives of another.

30 in every stage of these oppressions we have petitioned for redress in the most humble

31 terms; our repeated petitions have been answered by repeated injury. a prince

32 whose character is thus marked by every act which may define a tyrant, is unfit

33 to be the ruler of a people who mean to be free. future ages will scarce believe

34 that the hardiness of one man, adventured within the short compass of ~~12~~ *twelve* years

35 only, on so many acts of tyranny without a mask, over a people fostered & fixed in principles

36 of liberty.

1   Nor have we been wanting in attentions to our British brethren. we have

2   warned them from time to time of attempts by their legislature to extend a juris-

3   -diction over these our states. we have reminded them of the circumstances of

4   our emigration & settlement here, no one of which could warrant so strange a

5   pretension: that these were effected at the expence of our own blood & treasure,

6   unassisted by the wealth or the strength of Great Britain: that in constituting

7   indeed our several forms of government, we had adopted one common king, thereby

8   laying a foundation for perpetual league & amity with them: but that submission to their

9   parliament was no part of our constitution, nor ever in idea, if history may be

10   credited: and we appealed to their native justice & magnanimity, as well as to the ties

11   of our common kindred to disavow these usurpations which were likely to interrupt

12   our correspondence & connection. they too have been deaf to the voice of justice &

13   of consanguinity, & when occasions have been given them, by the regular course of

14   their laws, of removing from their councils the disturbers of our harmony, they

15   have by their free election re-established them in power. at this very time too they

16   are permitting their chief magistrate to send over not only soldiers of our common

17   blood, but Scotch & foreign mercenaries to invade & deluge us in blood. these facts

18   have given the last stab to agonizing affection and manly spirit bids us to re-

19   -nounce for ever these unfeeling brethren. we must endeavor to forget our former

20   love for them, and to hold them as we hold the rest of mankind, enemies in war,

21   in peace friends. we might have been a free & a great people together; but a commu-

22   -nication of grandeur & of freedom it seems is below their dignity. be it so, since they

23   will have it; the road to ~~glory &~~ happiness *& to glory* is open to us too; we will climb it ~~in~~

24   *apart from them* ~~a separate state,~~ and acquiesce in the necessity which ~~pro~~nounces our *de*~~ever-~~

25   ~~-lasting Adieu!~~ eternal separation!

26   We therefore the representatives of the United States of America in General Con-

27   -gress assembled do, in the name & by authority of the good people of these states,

28   reject and renounce all allegiance & subjection to the kings of Great Britain

29   & all others who may hereafter claim by, through, or under them; we utterly

30   dissolve & break off all political connections which may have heretofore sub-

31   -sisted between us & the people or parliament of Great Britain; and finally

32   we do assert and declare these colonies to be free and independant states,

33   and that as free & independant states they shall hereafter have power to levy

34   war, conclude peace, contract alliances, establish commerce, & to do all other

35   acts and things which independant states may of right do. And for the

36   support of this declaration we mutually pledge to each other our lives, our

37   fortunes, & our sacred honour.

Left: *Reconstruction of the fourth page of the Declaration as John Adams saw it.*

Jefferson kept fiddling with the next-to-last paragraph right up to the time he showed it to Adams. He copied the passage from the original draft (see page 37), then made the four changes (lines 23, 24, 25), and, for some reason, went back and recorded them on his work sheet.

Denounce, in our era, has lost the meaning *pronounce, which it had in Jefferson's day (line 24). The substitution of* eternal separation *for* everlasting Adieu *(line 25), eliminated a French word that did not sound serious enough for the occasion.*

Left, overleaf: *First page of John Adams's copy of the Declaration written in his own hand.* (Library of Congress) Right, overleaf: *Reconstruction.*

This is an important document, as it serves as a guidepost for separating the layers of changes in the Rough Draft (see page vii). By comparing this with the first page of the Rough Draft as it looked when Jefferson was ready to submit the Declaration to Congress (page 78), it is clear that Adams made this copy long before Jefferson had finished his rewriting.

As Adams's change of his Majesty *to* the King of Great Britain *(line 26) does not appear here, he must have suggested this change to Jefferson after he made this copy. That the change was Adams's, we know from a notation Jefferson later put in the left-hand margin of the Rough Draft (page 78).*

Any changes that Adams incorporated in his copy must have been made by Jefferson before Adams saw the Declaration. Sacred & undeniable, *for example, must have already been changed to* self evident *(line 7).*

59

A Declaration by the Representatives of the United States of America in general Congress assembled

When in the Course of human Events it becomes necessary for a People to advance from that Subordination, in which they have hitherto remained and to assume among the Powers of the Earth, the equal and independent Station to which the Laws of Nature and of Nature's God entitle them, a decent Respect to the opinions of Mankind requires that they should declare the Causes, which impell them to the Change.

We hold these Truths to be self evident; that all Men are created equal and independent; that from that equal Creation they derive Rights inherent and unalienable; among which are the Preservation of Life, and Liberty, and the Pursuit of Happiness; that to secure these Ends, Governments are instituted among Men, deriving their just Powers from the Consent of the governed; that whenever, any form of Government, shall become destructive of these Ends, it is the Right of the People to alter, or to abolish it, and to institute new Government, laying its Foundation on such Principles, and organising its Powers in such Form, as to them shall seem most likely to effect their Safety, and Happiness. Prudence indeed will dictate that Governments long established should not be changed for light and transient Causes: and accordingly all Experience hath shewn, that Mankind are more disposed to suffer, while Evils are sufferable, than to right themselves, by abolishing the Forms to which they are accustomed. But when a long Train of Abuses and Usurpations, begun at a distinguish'd Period, and pursuing invariably, the same Object, evinces a Design to reduce them under absolute Power, it is their Right, it is their Duty, to throw off such Government, and to provide new Guards for their future Security. Such has been the patient Sufferance of these Colonies; and such is now the Necessity, which constrains them to expunge their former Systems of Government. The History of his present Majesty, is a History, of unremitting Injuries and Usurpations, among which no one Fact stands single or solitary to contradict the uniform Tenor of the rest, all of which have in direct Object, the Establishment of an absolute Tyranny over these States. To prove this, let Facts be submitted to a candid World, for the Truth of which We pledge a Faith, as yet unsullied by Falshood.

A Declaration by the Representatives of the
UNITED STATES OF AMERICA *in general Congress assembled*

1 When in the Course of human Events it becomes necessary for a People

2 to advance from that Subordination, in which they have hitherto remained

3 and to assume among the Powers of the Earth, the equal and independent Station

4 to which the Laws of Nature and of Nature's God entitle them, a decent

5 Respect to the opinions of Mankind requires that they should declare the

6 Causes, which impell them to the Change.

7 We hold these Truths to be Self evident; that all Men are created equal

8 and independent; that from that equal Creation they derive Rights inherent

9 and unalienable; among which are the Preservation of Life, and Liberty, and the

10 Pursuit of Happiness; that to secure these Ends, Governments are instituted

11 among Men, deriving their just Powers from the Consent of the governed; that

12 whenever, any form of Government, shall become destructive of these Ends,

13 it is the Right of the People to alter, or to abolish it, and to institute new Go-

14 vernment, laying its Foundation on such Principles, and organizing its Powers

15 in such Form, as to them shall seem most likely to effect their Safety

16 and Happiness. Prudence indeed will dictate that Governments long established

17 should not be changed for light and transient Causes: and accordingly all

18 Experience hath shewn, that Mankind are more disposed to suffer, while Evils

19 are Sufferable, than to right themselves, by abolishing the Forms to which they

20 are accustomed. But when a long Train of Abuses and Usurpations, begun at

21 a distinguish'd Period, and pursuing invariably, the same Object, evinces a Design

22 to reduce them under absolute Power, it is their Right, it is their Duty, to throw

23 off such Government, and to provide new Guards for their future Security. Such

24 has been the patient sufferance of these Colonies; and such is now the Necessity

25 which constrains them to expunge their former Systems of Government. The History

26 of his present Majesty, is a History, of unremitting Injuries and Usurpations,

27 among which no one Fact stands Single or Solitary to contradict the uniform

28 Tenor of the rest, all of which have in direct object, the Establishment of an

29 absolute Tyranny over these States. To prove this, let Facts be submitted to a

30 candid World, for the Truth of which We pledge a Faith, as yet unsullied by

31 Falsehood.

CHAPTER TEN

Jefferson's Virginia

It was now the evening of Thursday, June 20. The High Street market stalls were empty, but lots of horses were tied up outside the taverns, flicking their tails at the big flies that settled on their rumps. Perhaps, at the India Queen Tavern, Jefferson dropped the declaration off with Roger Sherman of Connecticut. (We have no record of what Sherman or Robert Livingston said about the draft or if they made any changes, but as members of the committee they must have seen it.)

Back on his horse, Jefferson passed the crowd smoking outside another inn, the India King, and the New York stagecoach as it rumbled into Bank Street. A great cloud of sea gulls flapped mewing into the air from the garbage beside the courthouse; and beggars hooted at him from the city jail, stretching bare hands through the bars.

Later, Bob Hemings led the horses away to Hiltzheimer's stables. As the last rays of the sun slanted across the boy's face, Jefferson thought he noticed a trace of his beloved Patty, Bob's half-sister. Observing the resemblance, Jefferson felt, more deeply than usual, the hardship of separation.

Jefferson and Patty had been married four and a half years. In 1772, Patty, Martha Wayles Skelton, had been a widow of twenty-three, and Thomas had been a bachelor of twenty-nine. Now she was twenty-seven and he was thirty-three. If it were not for the war, he would be finishing his great house, Monticello, on his estate on the Rivanna River. Instead, he was alone in Philadelphia while his pregnant wife and their three-and-a-half-year-old daughter Patsy stayed with Patty's sister, Elizabeth, near the Virginia coast, threatened by British warships.

Patty had already lost two children: her son by her first husband and her little daughter Jane by Jefferson. It was hard enough being a woman in those days without being deserted for months at a time. Some wives, losing too many children, went mad. More died in childbirth.

The war was taking away their years together. Jefferson reluctantly remained

Another view of Philadelphia, a few blocks from where John Adams stayed in 1776. (Library of Congress)

in Philadelphia, but it would only be for a little while—until August 10, the end of his one-year term.

Jefferson's political life pulled him to Philadelphia. His private life pulled him to Virginia. The strength of the pull to Virginia can be seen by the fact that he had been away from the Congress for four-and-a-half eventful months that prepared the way for the colonies' independence. From the end of December 1775 until the middle of May 1776, the other members of Congress had struggled with setting up navy and war departments (standing committees), with the campaign in Canada, and the beginnings of foreign affairs, asking Monsieur Archard Bonvouloir, secret agent of France, for arms, ammunition, and the help of the French navy.

While all this was going on, Jefferson had been immersed in his Virginia world of estates and slaves. He owned many plantations: Monticello, Shadwell, Tuftons, Pouncey's, Portobello, Bear Creek, and Lego in Albemarle County; and the Poplar Forest, Wingo's, Judith's Creek, Crank's, Elk Hill, India Camp, Angola, Guinea, Bridge Quarter, Liggons, and other farms, fields, and wooded tracts in Bedford and Campbell counties—10,000 acres, 15 square miles in all, and a 215-foot-high natural stone arch spanning a creek. He spent his days riding horses from one tract to another, trotting through the Poplar Forest, directing the planting of trees and shrubs at Monticello.

There were endless details: the making of bricks, the mending of fences, the purchasing of salt pork and fish for the slaves, the distribution of clothes and blankets, the planning of crops. He prepared a census of the "number of souls in my family in Albemarle":

	free	slave
males of 16 yrs old & upwds	17	22
females ″ ″ ″ ″	5	17
males below 16	4	22
females below 16	8	22
number of free & slaves	34	83
number in the whole 117		

There were 83 slaves in Albemarle and 104 more in Bedford and Campbell.

Jefferson had been gone so long and shown so little interest in affairs of state that even some of his friends on the Virginia delegation had begun to doubt his attachment to the cause.

He had been ready to leave Monticello in the middle of March when his mother's sudden death precipitated a crisis. He suffered terrible migraine headaches every day for six weeks, which kept him in Virginia longer. The reason for this very painful kind of mourning can only be guessed at. Little is known of Jefferson's mother, Martha Randolph Jefferson. None of her letters have survived. From various comments Thomas made it would seem that he had little respect for her. His mother, with many close relatives in England, may have disapproved of her son's politics. If so, once his headaches were gone, her death may have left Jefferson freer to pursue his revolutionary activities.

As the time for submitting the Declaration to Congress drew near, Jefferson continued worrying over the first page. He was still not satisfied with it.

When in the course of human events it becomes necessary for a people to

advance from that subordination in which they have hitherto remained, & to as-

separate and equal
-sume among the powers of the earth the equal & independant station to

which the laws of nature & of nature's god entitle them, a decent respect

to the opinions of mankind requires that they should declare the causes

which impel them to the change.

self evident
We hold these truths to be sacred & undeniable; that all men are

they are endowed by their creator with
created equal & independant, that from that equal creation they derive

rights
rights inherent & inalienable, among which are the preservation of

life, & liberty & the pursuit of happiness; that to secure these ends go-

He could only hope that others appreciated his meanings. The fate of his words was in their hands.

CHAPTER ELEVEN

Benjamin Franklin, Editor

There are several reasons for believing that Benjamin Franklin saw the Declaration after John Adams and not before:

1) None of the changes that Jefferson said were made by Franklin are in the copy that Adams made for himself.

2) One of the changes that Adams made can be shown to have been made before Franklin made one of the changes that Jefferson attributes to him. On line 23 of the first page of the Rough Draft (page 78), *to arbitrary power* has been changed to *under absolute Despotism*. In a note in the margin of the Rough Draft, Jefferson gives Franklin credit for the entire change, saying it is in "Dr. Franklin's handwriting." Professor Julian Boyd points out, however, that the words *under absolute* and *Despotism* were written at different times (note how much darker *Despotism* is) and probably by different hands. For one thing, *absolute* in line 23 looks almost exactly like *absolute* in the third line from the bottom. This indicates that the words *under absolute* are in Jefferson's handwriting. *Despotism* very likely is in Franklin's handwriting. The capital *D* is different from Jefferson's (see *Declaration* in the title) as is the *m* at the end of the word (see *them*, line 4, or *form*, line 12).

Further evidence that these words were not written at the same time is found in Adams's copy of the Declaration (page 60). In line 22 of the first page of his copy, he has *under absolute Power* instead of *under absolute Despotism*. It looks as if, at the time Adams made his copy, *to arbitrary power* had been changed to *under absolute power* as he has it. *Power* (Adams capitalized the noun) became *Despotism* later. If it is true that Jefferson changed the first two words and Franklin was only responsible for changing *power* to *Despotism*, then Adams must have made his copy before Franklin made his change.

Assuming this reasoning to be correct, and that Franklin saw the document after Adams, when did Franklin see it? The insertion of *Scotch &*, in *Scotch & foreign mercenaries*, gives June 18 as the earliest date that Adams could have seen the Rough Draft. We have assumed that Adams did not see it until the 19th. Adams kept it long enough not only to carefully review it, but to make a copy in his own handwriting. He could have returned it to Jefferson any time after the morning of the 19th. We have assumed that he kept it until the 20th. The Declaration was presented to Congress on the 28th. Franklin, then, could have seen it at any time between the 20th and the 28th. Are there any clues as to exactly when he did see it?

There exists a letter from Jefferson to Franklin referring to a paper that Jefferson wishes the older man to go over (see page 68). The letter bears no real dateline, only the notation "Friday morn." As Jefferson and Franklin served on a number of committees that prepared papers in 1775 and 1776, the letter could refer to any document that was being worked on over a Friday by one of the committees on which they both served. By a process of elimination, most scholars agree that the paper most probably refers to the Declaration of Independence. If this is so, to which Friday does it refer? The committee of five was selected on Tuesday, June 11 and the Declaration was presented to Congress on Friday, June 28. There were three Fridays during which the committee was working: June 14, June 21, and June 28. June 14 can be eliminated because Jefferson did not complete his original draft until the 18th at the earliest. June 28 can be eliminated because the document was handed in on that day, and the note to Franklin alludes to a *further* meeting of the committee. This leaves only Friday, June 21.

Benjamin Franklin was staying at a stone farmhouse several miles outside of Philadelphia. The oldest member of Congress, the seventy-year-old Franklin was recovering from a two-month mission to Canada, much of which had been spent in ice and snow, sleeping on flatboats beneath canvas awnings. He had not been in the city since before Jefferson's committee was formed, and had been taking little part in the business of either the Continental Congress or the Pennsylvania convention that was planning to overthrow the existing royal government of the colony.

It was a difficult time for Franklin. On top of his weariness, he had the gout so badly that he could barely walk. And he had just heard that the new New Jersey provincial (rebel) assembly had arrested his son William, the colony's royal governor. It was an unusual case—an old man a rebel, with a son on the side of tradition!

No man in Pennsylvania knew better than Franklin what was happening. He had spent sixteen of the past eighteen years in England as agent for the Pennsylvania Assembly. He knew better than anyone in the colonies the true thinking of the British ministry, and the currents of opinion prevailing in London. The famous peace plan of William Pitt, Lord Chatham, had been shown to Franklin before it was submitted to the House of Lords in January 1775. Chatham had spent hours in Franklin's lodgings, explaining his plan to have Parliament suspend the laws the

Americans did not like and recognize the Continental Congress as an American Parliament.

Because he had witnessed the defeat of Chatham's plan, as well as the popularity of Lord North's punitive measures, Franklin knew that there was no hope of reconciliation and that independence was the only sensible course. He had spent a long evening after his return arguing this with his son William and with Joseph Galloway, the man who had replaced Franklin as a leader of the Pennsylvania assembly. Sadly, he had not convinced either.

Now, in Benfield, the stone farmhouse of his friend, the clockmaker Edward Duffield, far from the turmoil of the Pennsylvania State House, the old man may have wondered who was right. Things had gone badly in Canada, an enormous British fleet was on its way to attack the colonies, and in the South, British marauders were threatening to ignite a slave rebellion. In another six months perhaps, William Franklin would be free and his father imprisoned. And all this business of Congress, so necessary, so endless, kept the elder Franklin from interests closer to his heart: the unearthing of huge mysterious bones, the puzzles of electricity and head colds, the classification of plants, and the sea. (On his voyage home from England the previous year, he had lowered a thermometer into the ocean four times a day, trying to locate the path of the Gulf Stream. He had seen that it might be understood as a river—a startling idea that would not be rediscovered for many years.)

Opening Jefferson's envelope, Franklin thought about its sender: thin, sandy-haired, with a clever, freckled face. Jefferson was the kind who had to write before he spoke, to carefully compose his thoughts. Franklin had served with him on the committee that drafted the 1775 Declaration of Causes and he had seen how Jefferson suffered over Dickinson's suggestions. Franklin knew as much about writing as any man in Congress, having made his living as printer, publisher, editor, and author. And of all the forms of literary endeavor, none, he knew, was more unpleasant than writing for a committee. One of the benefits of age was that Franklin could decline such duties.

The old man put on his spectacles, readjusted his leg—extended to relieve the gout pain in his big toe—and began reading. With the four-page declaration was a brief note from Jefferson:

Th. J. to DOCTOR FRANKLYN *Friday morn.*

The inclosed paper has been read and with some small alterations approved of by the committee. Will Doctr. Franklyn be so good as to peruse it and suggest such alterations as his more enlarged view of the subject will dictate? The paper having been returned to me to change a particular sentiment or two, I propose laying it again before the committee tomorrow morning, if Doctr. Franklyn can think of it before that time.

Franklin began to read the paper:

A Declaration by the Representatives of the United States of America, in General Congress Assembled.
When in the course of human events . . .

He would, Dr. Franklin decided, leave it to others to correct the grammar and spelling: *independant* for *independent, unacknoleged* for *unacknowledged*; the quaint use of lowercase letters at the beginnings of sentences and even in the words *god* and *parliament*; the introduction of the apostrophe in *it's*; the haphazard use of the ampersand (&) and the word *and*; of colons and semi-colons. It was the wording that was important. But he would tread lightly on Jefferson.

Assuming Franklin received the document on the 21st, we can assume that, following the instructions in the letter, he returned it promptly. The following morning, Saturday, June 22, Jefferson found that Franklin had made just seven changes.

Left, overleaf: Reconstruction of the first page of the Declaration as Franklin saw it, and with his changes circled.

Jefferson definitely attributed the substitution of Despotism *for* power *(line 23) to Franklin. This is very important, because a close examination of the Rough Draft (page 78) indicates that this change was made after* under absolute *was substituted for* to arbitrary. *Since Adams's copy reads* under absolute Power, *this is a clue to the fact that Adams saw the document before Franklin. Handwriting clues also indicate that Franklin made the other two changes attributed to him on this page. One (line 1) certainly makes the first sentence stronger, and* separation *(line 6) is more specific and emphatic than* change. *This last alteration seems to have gone through two stages. If you look carefully at the photograph of the first page of the Rough Draft (page 78) you can see that* separation *was originally* separate, *and that the* e *had the* i *of* ion *written over it. Franklin must first have changed* impel them to the change *to* impel them to separate; *and then altered it further to* impel them to the separation. *This explains why he had to insert* the *between the lines, instead of using the original* the.

by
A Declaration ~~of~~ the Representatives of the
UNITED STATES OF AMERICA, *in General Congress assembled.*

1   When in the course of human events it becomes necessary for ~~a~~ (one) people to

2   advance from that subordination in which they have hitherto remained, & to as-

separate and equal
3   -sume among the powers of the earth the ~~equal & independant~~ station to

4   which the laws of nature & of nature's god entitle them, a decent respect

5   to the opinions of mankind requires that they should declare the causes

the
6   which impel them to ~~the change.~~ (separation.)

self evident
7   We hold these truths to be ~~sacred & undeniable;~~ that all men are

they are endowed by their creator with
8   created equal & independant, that ~~from that equal creation they derive~~

rights
9   ~~rights~~ inherent & inalienable , among which are the preservation of

10   life, & liberty & the pursuit of happiness; that to secure these ends, go-

11   -vernments are instituted among men, deriving their just powers from

12   the consent of the governed; that whenever any form of government

13   shall become destructive of these ends, it is the right of the people to alter

14   or to abolish it, & to institute new government, laying it's foundation on

15   such principles & organising it's powers in such form, as to them shall

16   seem most likely to effect their safety & happiness. prudence indeed

17   will dictate that governments long established should not be changed for

18   light & transient causes: and accordingly all experience hath shewn that

19   mankind are more disposed to suffer while evils are sufferable, than to

20   right themselves by abolishing the forms to which they are accustomed. but

21   when a long train of abuses & usurpations, begun at a distinguished period,

22   & pursuing invariably the same object, evinces a design to ~~subject~~ reduce

under absolute (Despotism)
23   them ~~to arbitrary power,~~ it is their right, it is their duty, to throw off such

24   government & to provide new guards for their future security. such has

25   been the patient sufferance of these colonies; & such is now the necessity

26   which constrains them to expunge their former systems of government.

the   *King of Great Britain*
27   the history of ~~his~~ present ~~majesty,~~ is a history of unremitting injuries and

28   usurpations, among which no one fact stands single or solitary to contra-

29   -dict the uniform tenor of the rest, all of which have in direct object the

30   establishment of an absolute tyranny over these states. to prove this, let facts be

31   submitted to a candid world, for the truth of which we pledge a faith

32   yet unsullied by falsehood.

Benjamin Franklin as he appeared two years after the drafting of the Declaration. He was painted by Joseph Duplessis in 1778, while serving as Congress's envoy in Paris. (The Metropolitan Museum of Art, Bequest of Michael Friedsam, 1932, The Michael Friedsam Collection)

Right: *Reconstruction of the second page of the Declaration as Franklin saw it, and with his changes circled.*

Franklin's change on line 22 sharpened the charge. The King didn't just set the salaries of judges, he decided when they would be paid.
As the British saw it, many of these complaints were absurd. According to their constitution, the King had a perfect right to veto laws (lines 1 to 5), to dissolve legislatures (lines 7 to 11), and to appoint judges (lines 19 to 22).
On the other hand, the charges on lines 25, 26, 29–31, referred to practices that no Englishman would tolerate. King Charles I had quartered troops among his subjects, and the English Civil War (1642–1649) broke out after he used military forces against civilians.
The others with whom the King combines (line 27) are Parliament. This is the only reference to Parliament that would remain in the document by the time Congress finished with it.
Notice that Jefferson had altered the change Adams had made on line 11: long space of time *has become simply* long time, *the same meaning in two fewer words.*

1   he has refused his assent to laws the most wholesome and necessary for the pub-

2   -lic good:

3   he has forbidden his governors to pass laws of immediate & pressing importance,

4   unless suspended in their operation till his assent should be obtained;

5   and when so suspended, he has neglected utterly to attend to them.

6   he has refused to pass other laws for the accomodation of large districts of people

7   unless those people would relinquish the right of representation; a right *in the legislature*

8   inestimable to them & formidable to tyrants ~~alone:~~ *only*

9   he has dissolved Representative houses repeatedly & continually, for opposing with

10   manly firmness his invasions on the rights of the people:

11   he has refused for a long ~~space of time~~ to cause others to be elected, *time after such Dissolutions*

12   whereby the legislative powers, incapable of annihilation, have returned to

13   the people at large for their exercise, the state remaining in the mean time

14   exposed to all the dangers of invasion from without & convulsions within:

15   he has endeavored to prevent the population of these states; for that purpose

16   obstructing the laws for naturalization of foreigners; refusing to pass others

17   to encourage their migrations hither; & raising the conditions of new ap-

18   -propriations of lands:

19   he has suffered the administration of justice totally to cease in some of these

20   ~~colonies,~~ refusing his assent to laws for establishing judiciary powers: *states*

21   he has made our judges dependant on his will alone, for the tenure of their offices,

22   and amount of their salaries: *(the)* *(& payment)*

23   he has erected a multitude of new offices by a self-assumed power, & sent hi-

24   -ther swarms of officers to harrass our people & eat out their substance:

25   he has kept among us in times of peace standing armies & ships of war:

26   he has affected to render the military, independant of & superior to the civil power:

27   he has combined with others to subject us to a jurisdiction foreign to our constitu-

28   -tions and unacknoleged by our laws; giving his assent to their pretended acts

29   of legislation, for quartering large bodies of armed troops among us;

30   for protecting them by a mock-trial from punishment for any murders

31   they should commit on the inhabitants of these states;

32   for cutting off our trade with all parts of the world;

33   for imposing taxes on us without our consent;

34   for depriving us of the benefits of trial by jury;

35   for transporting us beyond seas to be tried for pretended offences;

valuable

abolishing our most ~~important~~ *Laws*

1   for taking away our charters, & altering fundamentally the forms of our governments;

2   for suspending our own legislatures & declaring themselves invested with power to

3   legislate for us in all cases whatsoever.

4   he has abdicated government here, withdrawing his governors, & declaring us out

5   of his allegiance & protection:

6   he has plundered our seas, ravaged our coasts, burnt our towns & destroyed the

7   lives of our people;

8   he is at this time transporting large armies of foreign mercenaries to compleat

9   the works of death, desolation & tyranny, already begun with circumstances

10   of cruelty & perfidy unworthy the head of a civilized nation:

11 he has endeavored to bring on the inhabitants of our frontiers the merciless Indian

12   savages, whose known rule of warfare is an undistinguished destruction of

13   all ages, sexes, & conditions of existence:

citizens

14 he has incited treasonable insurrections of our fellow-~~subjects~~, with the

15   allurements of forfeiture & confiscation of our property:

16 he has waged cruel war against human nature itself, violating it's most sa-

17   -cred rights of life & liberty in the persons of distant people who never of-

18   -fended him, captivating & carrying them into slavery in another hemi-

19   -sphere, or to incur miserable death in their transportation thither. this

20   piratical warfare, the opprobrium of infidel powers, is the warfare of the

21   Christian king of Great Britain. [determined to keep open a market

22   where MEN should be bought & sold,] he has prostituted his negative

23   for suppressing every legislative attempt to prohibit or to restrain this

determining to keep open a market where MEN should be bought & sold

24 execrable commerce: and that this assemblage of horrors might want no fact

25   of distinguished die, he is now exciting those very people to rise in arms

26   among us, and to purchase that liberty of which he has deprived them,

27   by murdering the people upon whom he also obtruded them; thus paying

28   off former crimes committed against the liberties of one people, with crimes

29   which he urges them to commit against the lives of another.

30 in every stage of these oppressions we have petitioned for redress in the most humble

only

31 terms; our repeated petitions have been answered by repeated injury. a prince

32   whose character is thus marked by every act which may define a tyrant, is unfit

33   to be the ruler of a people who mean to be free. future ages will scarce believe

twelve

34 that the hardiness of one man, adventured within the short compass of ~~12~~ years

35   only, on so many acts of tyranny without a mask, over a people fostered & fixed in principles

36   of liberty.

1   Nor have we been wanting in attentions to our British brethren. we have

2   warned them from time to time of attempts by their legislature to extend a juris-

3   -diction over these our states. we have reminded them of the circumstances of

4   our emigration & settlement here, no one of which could warrant so strange a

5   pretension: that these were effected at the expence of our own blood & treasure,

6   unassisted by the wealth or the strength of Great Britain: that in constituting

7   indeed our several forms of government, we had adopted one common king, thereby

8   laying a foundation for perpetual league & amity with them: but that submission to *their*

9   parliament was no part of our constitution, nor ever in idea, if history may be

10   credited: and we appealed to their native justice & magnanimity, as well as to the ties

11   of our common kindred to disavow these usurpations which were likely to interrupt

12   our correspondence & connection. they too have been deaf to the voice of justice &

13   of consanguinity, & when occasions have been given them, by the regular course of

14   their laws, of removing from their councils the disturbers of our harmony, they

15   have by their free election re-established them in power. at this very time too they

16   are permitting their chief magistrate to send over not only soldiers of our common

destroy us

17   blood, but Scotch & foreign mercenaries to invade & ~~deluge us in blood.~~ these facts

18   have given the last stab to agonizing affection and manly spirit bids us to re-

19   -nounce for ever these unfeeling brethren. we must endeavor to forget our former

20   love for them, and to hold them as we hold the rest of mankind, enemies in war,

21   in peace friends. we might have been a free & a great people together; but a commu-

22   -nication of grandeur & of freedom it seems is below their dignity. be it so, since they

& to glory

23   will have it; the road to ~~glory &~~ happiness ∧ is open to us too; we will climb it ~~in~~

apart from them   *de*

24   ~~a separate state,~~ and acquiesce in the necessity which ~~pro~~nounces our ~~ever-~~

25   ~~-lasting Adieu!~~ eternal separation!

26   We therefore the representatives of the United States of America in General Con-

27   -gress assembled do, in the name & by authority of the good people of these states,

28   reject and renounce all allegiance & subjection to the kings of Great Britain

29   & all others who may hereafter claim by, through, or under them; we utterly

30   dissolve & break off all political connections which may have heretofore sub-

31   -sisted between us & the people or parliament of Great Britain; and finally

32   we do assert and declare these colonies to be free and independant states,

33   and that as free & independant states they shall hereafter have power to levy

34   war, conclude peace, contract alliances, establish commerce, & to do all other

35   acts and things which independant states may of right do. And for the

36   support of this declaration we mutually pledge to each other our lives, our

37   fortunes, & our sacred honour.

Reconstruction of the fourth page of the Declaration as Franklin saw it, and with his changes circled.

In the one change Franklin made on this page (line 17), he had, without knowing it, restored the simpler wording Jefferson had first written. Franklin had made a total of seven changes on the four pages.

75

In their first inspections of the Declaration, Adams and Franklin had made just ten changes, half on Jefferson's precious first page, and had suggested one additional charge against the King.

Jefferson, working with Adams and possibly with the other three members of the committee, added Adams's new charge as well as two others, and made nineteen more alterations in wording in addition to the ten suggested by Adams and Franklin on their first readings.

The new phrases on the first page had a cadence that was missing in those they replaced, giving the sentences the easy flow of good writing, in which sound and sense join together.

But what was this sense? We cannot be certain that we know exactly what these phrases meant to people in 1776. Words change their meanings over the years. (We would never use *distinguished* today the way Jefferson used it as a synonym for *definite*.)

Remembering that many of the delegates owned slaves and were wealthy, we can sense that their love of freedom was not separate from their own desire for power. It was the wealthy barons of England who forced *Magna Carta*, the first document of freedom, on King John in 1215, not the commoners. On his plantations in Virginia, Jefferson was a kind of king, intolerant of any other monarch's efforts to deprive him of anything.

If Locke's *life, liberty and property* became in Jefferson's hands *life, & liberty & the pursuit of happiness*, it was not because Jefferson valued *property* the less, but because he had learned that more fundamental than property itself was the right of deciding how to use it. Jefferson had been a member of Virginia's legislature, its House of Burgesses, where he enjoyed the right of passing laws and making decisions that shaped life in the colony of Virginia.

Other Virginians, farmers of their own land, could at least vote on who represented them in the legislature. In the northern colonies there were even more opportunities for such enjoyment. In New England alone, there were more than five hundred town meetings, general courts, and other municipal bodies in which independent farmers, merchants, and prosperous craftsmen governed their own affairs. It may have been of this kind of enjoyment that Jefferson and the other members of Congress thought when they read *happiness* in *the pursuit of happiness*. Perhaps happiness was the right of having a say in one's destiny, which included taking part in decisions that affected one's property. (It did not mean, as some have since taken it to mean, merely the right to have a good time.)

And what did they think of when they read that *all men are created equal?* Did they mean that they, themselves, were equal to the 160,000 electors of the British Parliament, or that their own servants and slaves were equal to them?

Left, overleaf: *First page of Rough Draft of the Declaration in Jefferson's own hand*. (Library of Congress) Right, overleaf: *Type reconstruction showing the changes (circled) made by Jefferson after showing it to Adams and before and after showing it to Franklin.*

The Rough Draft is the source of most of what is known about how Jefferson wrote the Declaration. It is a record of all the stages except the earliest work-sheet stage (pages 2 and 34), up to the time the Declaration was submitted to Congress.

Careful study of the Rough Draft reveals many items of interest. At some point Jefferson put brackets around the passages deleted by Congress; and many years later (lines 23 and 27) he noted the changes made by Franklin and Adams.

Notice (line 22) the way the substitute word reduce *comes exactly at the end of the line. This shows that Jefferson made this change as he was copying from a previous draft. If he had made the change after the page was copied, the line would have ended with* them to *and he would have had to put* reduce *in the space above* subject.

The fact that Jefferson started line 9 with in *and crossed it out is another sign that he was copying from a previous draft. He must have thought he had written* rights *at the end of line 8, and was starting to write* inherent *when he saw his error.*

With its ideas of revolution, this first page is by far the most interesting part of the Declaration. That Jefferson spent more time on it than on any other page can be seen from the fact that he made thirteen changes, more than on all the other pages put together.

Some of the most memorable phrases came in rewriting: dissolve the political bands *(line 2)*, separate and equal *(line 3)*, endowed by their creator *(line 8)*.

A Declaration by the Representatives of the UNITED STATES OF AMERICA, in General Congress assembled.

When in the course of human events it becomes necessary for one people to dissolve the political bands which have connected them with another, and to assume among the powers of the earth the separate and equal station to which the laws of nature & of nature's god entitle them, a decent respect to the opinions of mankind requires that they should declare the causes which impel them to the separation.

We hold these truths to be self-evident; that all men are created equal, that they are endowed by their creator with inherent & inalienable rights; that among these are life, & liberty, & the pursuit of happiness; that to secure these rights, governments are instituted among men, deriving their just powers from the consent of the governed; that whenever any form of government becomes destructive of these ends, it is the right of the people to alter or to abolish it, & to institute new government. laying it's foundation on such principles & organising it's powers in such form, as to them shall seem most likely to effect their safety & happiness. prudence indeed will dictate that governments long established should not be changed for light & transient causes: and accordingly all experience hath shewn that mankind are more disposed to suffer while evils are sufferable, than to right themselves by abolishing the forms to which they are accustomed. but when a long train of abuses & usurpations [begun at a distinguished period, &] pursuing invariably the same object, evinces a design to reduce them under absolute Despotism, it is their right, it is their duty. to throw off such & to provide new guards for their future security. such has been the patient sufferance of these colonies; & such is now the necessity which constrains them to expunge their former systems of government. the history of the present king of great Britain is a history of unremitting injuries and usurpations, [among which appears no solitary fact to contradict the uniform tenor of the rest, but all have] in direct object the establishment of an absolute tyranny over these states. to prove this, let facts be submitted to a candid world [for the truth of which we pledge a faith yet unsullied by falsehood]

Dr. Franklin's handwriting

mr Adams's hand writing

by
A Declaration ~~of~~ the Representatives of the
UNITED STATES OF AMERICA, *in General Congress assembled.*

one

1 When in the course of human events it becomes necessary for ~~a~~ people to
dissolve the political bands which have connected them with another, and to

2 ~~advance from that subordination in which they have hitherto remained, & to~~ as-
separate and equal

3 -sume among the powers of the earth the ~~equal & independant~~ station to

4 which the laws of nature & of nature's god entitle them, a decent respect

5 to the opinions of mankind requires that they should declare the causes

the

6 which impel them to ~~the change.~~ separation.

self evident

7 We hold these truths to be ~~sacred & undeniable;~~ that all men are

they are endowed by their creator with *equal*

8 created equal ~~& independant, that from that equal creation they derive~~
rights some of which are rights; *that* *these*

9 ~~rights~~ inherent & inalienable, among ~~which~~ are ~~the preservation of~~

rights

10 life, & liberty & the pursuit of happiness; that to secure these ~~ends,~~ go-

11 -vernments are instituted among men, deriving their just powers from

12 the consent of the governed; that whenever any form of government

13 *shall* becomes destructive of these ends, it is the right of the people to alter

14 or to abolish it, & to institute new government, laying it's foundation on

15 such principles & organising it's powers in such form, as to them shall

16 seem most likely to effect their safety & happiness. prudence indeed

17 will dictate that governments long established should not be changed for

18 light & transient causes: and accordingly all experience hath shewn that

19 mankind are more disposed to suffer while evils are sufferable, than to

20 right themselves by abolishing the forms to which they are accustomed. but

21 when a long train of abuses & usurpations, begun at a distinguished period,

22 & pursuing invariably the same object, evinces a design to ~~subject~~ reduce
under absolute Despotism

23 them ~~to arbitary power,~~ it is their right, it is their duty, to throw off such

24 government & to provide new guards for their future security. such has

25 been the patient sufferance of these colonies; & such is now the necessity

26 which constrains them to expunge their former systems of government.
the *King of Great Britain*

27 the history of ~~his~~ present ~~majesty,~~ is a history of unremitting injuries and
appears no solitary fact

28 usurpations, among which ~~no one fact stands single or solitary~~ to contra-
but all

29 -dict the uniform tenor of the rest, ~~all of which~~ have in direct object the

30 establishment of an absolute tyranny over these states. to prove this, let facts be

31 submitted to a candid world, for the truth of which we pledge a faith

32 yet unsullied by falsehood.

Left, overleaf: *The second page of the Rough Draft of the Declaration.* (Library of Congress) Right, overleaf: *Type reconstruction showing the changes (circled) made by Jefferson after showing it to Adams and Franklin.*

Notice Jefferson tried to insert without our consent *(line 25) after* peace, *before putting it at the end of the line. The new charge that follows line 35, added by Jefferson, refers to the King's permitting the French in Quebec to follow their old laws and customs. Another copying error appears on line 11, where Jefferson started writing* he has dissolved *(from line 9) instead of* he has refused. *The new charge inserted between lines 8 and 9 was probably suggested by John Adams, since it refers to an incident in Massachusetts in which the King ordered the legislature to meet in Cambridge instead of Boston. It does not appear in the photograph of the Rough Draft, but it was glued along the document's left-hand margin.*

he has refused his assent to laws the most wholesome and necessary for the pub-
-lic good:

he has forbidden his governors to pass laws of immediate & pressing importance,
   unless suspended in their operation till his assent should be obtained;
   and when so suspended, he has utterly neglected utterly to attend to them.

he has refused to pass other laws for the accomodation of large districts of people
   unless those people would relinquish the right of representation in the legislature, a right
   inestimable to them, & formidable to tyrants only:

as dissolved Repre~ ...tive houses repeatedly ...ants ... only

   ...ly firmness his invasions on the rights of the people:
   ~dissolved, he has refused for a long space of time time after such dissolutions to cause others to be elected,   * mr Adams
   whereby the legislative powers, incapable of annihilation, have returned to
   the people at large for their exercise, the state remaining in the mean time
   exposed to all the dangers of invasion from without, & convulsions within:

he has endeavored to prevent the population of these states; for that purpose
   obstructing the laws for naturalization of foreigners; refusing to pass others
   to encourage their migrations hither, & raising the conditions of new ap-
   -propriations of lands:

he has suffered the administration of justice totally to cease in some of these
   states refusing his assent to laws for establishing judiciary powers:

he has made [our] judges dependant on his will alone, for the tenure of their offices,
   the + & payment
   and amount of their salaries: + Dr Franklin

he has erected a multitude of new offices [by a self-assumed power,] & sent hi-
   -ther swarms of officers to harrass our people & eat out their substance:
he has kept among us in times of peace standing armies [& ships of war,] without the consent of our legislatures
he has affected to render the military, independent of & superior to the civil power:
he has combined with others to subject us to a jurisdiction foreign to ...
   -tions and unacknoleged by our laws; giving his assent to their acts of pretended
   of legislation, for quartering large bodies of armed troops among us;
      for protecting them by a mock-trial from punishment for any murders
      which
      they should commit on the inhabitants of these states;
      for cutting off our trade with all parts of the world;
      for imposing taxes on us without our consent;
      in many cases
      for depriving us of the benefits of trial by jury;
      for transporting us beyond seas to be tried for pretended offences:
      for abolishing the free system of English laws in a neighboring province, establishing therein an arbitrary government,
      and enlarging it's boundaries so as to render it at once an example & fit instrument for introducing the same ...
      ... to these colonies also:

1 he has refused his assent to laws the most wholesome and necessary for the pub-

2 -lic good:

3 he has forbidden his governors to pass laws of immediate & pressing importance,

4 unless suspended in their operation till his assent should be obtained;

5 and when so suspended, he has neglected utterly to attend to them.

6 he has refused to pass other laws for the accomodation of large districts of people

7 unless those people would relinquish the right of representation; a right *in the legislature*

8 inestimable to them & formidable to tyrants *only* ~~alone~~:

9 he has dissolved Representative houses repeatedly & continually, for opposing with

10 manly firmness his invasions on the rights of the people:

11 he has refused for a long ~~space of time~~ *time after such Dissolutions* to cause others to be elected,

12 whereby the legislative powers, incapable of annihilation, have returned to

13 the people at large for their exercise, the state remaining in the mean time

14 exposed to all the dangers of invasion from without, & convulsions within:

15 he has endeavored to prevent the population of these states; for that purpose

16 obstructing the laws for naturalization of foreigners; refusing to pass others

17 to encourage their migrations hither; & raising the conditions of new ap-

18 -propriations of lands:

19 he has suffered the administration of justice totally to cease in some of these

20 ~~colonies,~~ *states* refusing his assent to laws for establishing judiciary powers:

21 he has made our judges dependant on his will alone, for the tenure of their offices,

22 and *the* amount *& payment* of their salaries:

23 he has erected a multitude of new offices by a self-assumed power, & sent hi-

24 -ther swarms of officers to harrass our people & eat out their substance:

he has called together legislative bodies at places unusual, uncomfortable, & distant from the depository of their public records, for the sole purpose of fatiguing them into compliance with his measures.

25 he has kept among us in times of peace ~~without our consent~~ standing armies & ships of war *without ~~our~~ consent of our legislatures* *the*:

26 he has affected to render the military, independant of & superior to the civil power:

27 he has combined with others to subject us to a jurisdiction foreign to our constitu-

28 -tions and unacknoleged by our laws; giving his assent to their pretended ~~acts~~ *acts of*

29 *of* legislation, for quartering large bodies of armed troops among us;

30 for protecting them by a mock-trial from punishment for any murders

31 *which* they should commit on the inhabitants of these states;

32 for cutting off our trade with all parts of the world;

33 for imposing taxes on us without our consent;

34 for depriving us of the benefits of trial by jury;

35 for transporting us beyond seas to be tried for pretended offences:

for abolishing the free system of English laws in a neighboring province, establishing therein an arbitrary government and enlarging it's boundaries so as to render it at once an example & fit instrument for introducing the same absolute rule into these ~~colonies~~ states;

Left, overleaf: *The third page of the Rough Draft of the Declaration.* (Library of Congress) Right, overleaf: *Type reconstruction showing the changes (circled) made by Jefferson after showing it to Adams and Franklin.*

Notice in the photo of the Rough Draft that the first words of the charge that was inserted between lines 15 and 16, he has constrained, *also appear above line 11. Either Jefferson was thinking of putting the charge there, or began to write it in later, for above line 11, as we shall see, is where Congress decided to put it (page 115).*

Jefferson made one change on the Rough Draft even after Congress finished editing the Declaration. The alteration of injury *to* injuries *(line 31) appears neither in the official document as adopted by Congress nor in the copy Jefferson made for George Wythe on July 3 (page 99).*

From this edited Rough Draft, Jefferson probably made a neat copy to present to Congress. Unfortunately, that copy has been lost.

[†]abolishing our most ~~important~~ valuable Laws

for taking away our charters & altering fundamentally the forms of our governments,

for suspending our own legislatures & declaring themselves invested with power to

legislate for us in all cases whatsoever:

he has abdicated government here, [withdrawing his governors, & declaring us out
by declaring us out of his protection & waging war against us.

of his allegiance & protection:]

he has plundered our seas, ravaged our coasts, burnt our towns & destroyed the

lives of our people:

he is at this time transporting large armies of foreign mercenaries to compleat
Scotch and other

the works of ~~death, desolation~~ & tyranny, already begun with circumstances

of cruelty & perfidy ~~unworthy the head of a civilized nation:~~
scarcely paralleled in the most barbarous ages, and totally

he has ~~endeavored to bring on~~ the inhabitants of our frontiers the merciless Indian
he has ~~constrained~~ excited domestic insurrections amongst us, and has

savages, whose known rule of warfare is an undistinguished destruction of

all ages, sexes, & conditions [of existence:]

[he has incited treasonable insurrections of our fellow-~~citizens~~, with the

allurements of forfeiture & confiscation of our property:
he has ~~constrained others~~ ~~falling into the~~ ~~on the high seas to bear arms against~~ their country by taking

he has waged cruel war against human nature itself, violating it's most sa-

-cred rights of life & liberty in the persons of a distant people who never of-

-fended him, captivating & carrying them into slavery in another hemi-

-sphere, or to incur miserable death in their transportation thither. this

piratical warfare, the opprobrium of ~~infidel~~ powers, is the warfare of the

Christian king of Great Britain. determined to keep open a market

where MEN should be bought & sold he has prostituted his negative

for suppressing every legislative attempt to prohibit or to restrain this
~~determining to keep open a market where MEN should be bought & sold~~:

execrable commerce: and that this assemblage of horrors might want no fact

of distinguished die, he is now exciting those very people to rise in arms

among us, and to purchase that liberty of which he has deprived them,

~~by murdering the people~~ upon whom he also obtruded them: thus paying

off former crimes committed against the liberties of one people, with crimes

which he urges them to commit against the lives of another.]

in every stage of these oppressions" we have petitioned for redress in the most humble
only

terms; our repeated petitions have been answered by repeated injuries. a prince

whose character is thus marked by every act which may define a tyrant, is unfit
free

to be the ruler of a people [who mean to be free. future ages will scarce believe

that the hardiness of one man" adventured within the short compass of ~~twelve~~ years
to build a foundation so broad & undisguised" for tyranny

only", ~~over so many acts of tyranny without a mask~~, over a people fostered & fixed in principles

of ~~liberty~~ freedom]

valuable
abolishing our most ~~important~~ Laws

1   for taking away our charters, & altering fundamentally the forms of our governments;

2   for suspending our own legislatures & declaring themselves invested with power to

3   legislate for us in all cases whatsoever.

4   he has abdicated government here, withdrawing his governors, & declaring us out

5   of his allegiance & protection:

6   he has plundered our seas, ravaged our coasts, burnt our towns & destroyed the

7   lives of our people;

8   he is at this time transporting large armies of foreign mercenaries to compleat

9   the works of death, desolation & tyranny, already begun with circumstances

10   of cruelty & perfidy unworthy the head of a civilized nation:

11   he has endeavored to bring on the inhabitants of our frontiers the merciless Indian

12   savages, whose known rule of warfare is an undistinguished destruction of

13   all ages, sexes, & conditions of existence:

citizens
14   he has incited treasonable insurrections of our fellow-~~subjects~~, with the

15   allurements of forfeiture & confiscation of our property:

he has constrained others ~~falling into his hands~~ taken captive on the high seas to bear arms against their country ~~& to destroy & be destroyed by the brethren whom they love~~; to become the executioners of their friends & brethren or fall themselves by their hands:

16   he has waged cruel war against human nature itself, violating it's most sa-

17   -cred rights of life & liberty in the persons of distant people who never of-

18   -fended him, captivating & carrying them into slavery in another hemi-

19   -sphere, or to incur miserable death in their transportation thither. this

20   piratical warfare, the opprobrium of infidel powers, is the warfare of the

21   Christian king of Great Britain. [determined to keep open a market

22   where MEN should be bought & sold,] he has prostituted his negative

23   for suppressing every legislative attempt to prohibit or to restrain this

~~determining to keep open a market where MEN should be bought & sold~~
24   execrable commerce: and that this assemblage of horrors might want no fact

25   of distinguished die, he is now exciting those very people to rise in arms

26   among us, and to purchase that liberty of which he has deprived them,

27   by murdering the people upon whom he also obtruded them; thus paying

28   off former crimes committed against the liberties of one people, with crimes

29   which he urges them to commit against the lives of another.

30   in every stage of these oppressions we have petitioned for redress in the most humble

only
31   terms; our repeated petitions have been answered by repeated injury. a prince

32   whose character is thus marked by every act which may define a tyrant, is unfit

33   to be the ruler of a people who mean to be free. future ages will scarce believe

twelve
34   that the hardiness of one man, adventured within the short compass of ~~12~~ years

build
to ~~lay~~ a foundation so broad & undisguised, for tyranny
35   only, ~~on so many acts of tyranny without a mask~~, over a people fostered & fixed in principles

36   of ~~liberty.~~ freedom.

Left, overleaf: *The fourth page of the Rough Draft of the Declaration.* (Library of Congress) Right, overleaf: *Type reconstruction showing the changes (circled) made by Jefferson after showing it to Adams and Franklin.*

On line 24 Jefferson tried separately (adding an ly *to separate in* climb it separately) *before crossing the word out and inserting* apart from them. *In the photograph, notice the brackets on line 13 (& when . . .) and on line 24 (. . . apart from them, and). This, as we shall see, is one of the cuts made by Congress. Above line 13 Jefferson even inserted the change made by Congress to accommodate the cut:* We must therefore. *(He had first written it above* acquiesce *(line 24), then rubbed it out.)*

Nor have we been wanting in attentions to our British brethren. we have
warned them from time to time of attempts by their legislature to extend a juris-
                                                                    an unwarrantable
-diction over [these our states] we have reminded them of the circumstances of
our emigration & settlement here, [no one of which could warrant so strange a
pretension: that these were effected at the expence of our own blood & treasure,
unassisted by the wealth or the strength of Great Britain: that in constituting
indeed our several forms of government, we had adopted one common king, thereby
laying a foundation for perpetual league & amity with them: but that submission to their
~~parliament was no part of our constitution, nor ever in idea, if history may be~~
                                                                        & we have conjured them by
credited: and ~~we~~ have appealed to their native justice & magnanimity, [as well as to] the ties
                                                                  would inevitably
of our common kindred to disavow these usurpations which [were likely to] interrupt
   connection &
our correspondence ~~& connection~~.   they too have been deaf to the voice of justice &
                        we must therefore
of consanguinity. [& when occasions have been given them, by the regular course of
their laws, of removing from their councils the disturbers of our harmony, they]
have by their free election re-established them in power. at this very time too they
are permitting their chief magistrate to send over not only soldiers of our common
                                                        destroy us.
blood, but Scotch & foreign mercenaries to invade & ~~deluge us in blood~~ these facts
have given the last stab to agonizing affection, and manly spirit bids us to renounce for ever these unfeeling brethren. we must endeavor to forget our former
love for them, and to hold them as we hold the rest of mankind, enemies in war,
in peace friends. we might have been a free & a great people together; but a communication of grandeur & of freedom it seems is below their dignity. be it so, since they
                     ~~in blood~~   & to glory,   ~~must tread~~
will have it: the road to ~~happiness~~ & happiness, is open to us too; we will ~~climb~~ it ~~in~~
 apart from them,
~~a separate state~~, and [acquiesce in the necessity which ~~pronounces~~ our ~~everlasting~~
                                        de-
~~lasting Adieu~~! [eternal] separation! and hold them as we hold the rest of mankind, enemies in war, in peace friends.
    We therefore the representatives of the United States of America in General Con-
                    appealing to the supreme judge of the world for the rectitude of our intentions   colonies
-gress assembled, do, in the name & by authority of the good people of these [states]
reject & renounce all allegiance & subjection to the kings of Great Britain   a different phrase
                                                                                will be inserted
& all others who may hereafter claim by, through, or under them; & do utterly
                                                                have
dissolve ~~& break off~~ all political connection which may ~~have~~ heretofore subsisted
between us & the people or parliament of Great Britain; and finally
we do assert and declare these colonies to be free and independant states,
                                                          full
and that as free & independant states they ~~shall hereafter~~ have power to levy
war, conclude peace, contract alliances, establish commerce, & to do all other
acts and things which independant states may of right do. And for the
support of this declaration] we mutually pledge to each other our lives, our
fortunes, & our sacred honour.

independance declaration
original Rough draught

1   Nor have we been wanting in attentions to our British brethren. we have

2   warned them from time to time of attempts by their legislature to extend a juris-

3   -diction over these our states. we have reminded them of the circumstances of

4   our emigration & settlement here, no one of which could warrant so strange a

5   pretension: that these were effected at the expence of our own blood & treasure,

6   unassisted by the wealth or the strength of Great Britain: that in constituting

7   indeed our several forms of government, we had adopted one common king, thereby

8   laying a foundation for perpetual league & amity with them: but that submission to their

9   parliament was no part of our constitution, nor ever in idea, if history may be

10   credited: and we appealed to their native justice & magnanimity, as well as to the ties

11   of our common kindred to disavow these usurpations which were likely to interrupt

connection &

12   our ^ correspondence & connection. they too have been deaf to the voice of justice &

13   of consanguinity, & when occasions have been given them, by the regular course of

14   their laws, of removing from their councils the disturbers of our harmony, they

15   have by their free election re-established them in power. at this very time too they

16   are permitting their chief magistrate to send over not only soldiers of our common

destroy us

17   blood, but Scotch & foreign mercenaries to invade & deluge us in blood. these facts

18   have given the last stab to agonizing affection and manly spirit bids us to re-

19   -nounce for ever these unfeeling brethren. we must endeavor to forget our former

20   love for them, and to hold them as we hold the rest of mankind, enemies in war,

21   in peace friends. we might have been a free & a great people together; but a commu-

22   -nication of grandeur & of freedom it seems is below their dignity. be it so, since they

& to glory

23   will have it; the road to glory & happiness ^ is open to us too; we will climb it in

apart from them   *de*

24   a separately state, and acquiesce in the necessity which pronounces our ever-

25   -lasting Adieu! eternal separation!

26   We therefore the representatives of the United States of America in General Con-

27   -gress assembled do, in the name & by authority of the good people of these states,

28   reject and renounce all allegiance & subjection to the kings of Great Britain

29   & all others who may hereafter claim by, through, or under them; we utterly

have

30   dissolve & break off all political connection which may have heretofore ^ sub-

31   -sisted between us & the people or parliament of Great Britain; and finally

32   we do assert and declare these colonies to be free and independant states,

full

33   and that as free & independant states they shall hereafter have ^ power to levy

34   war, conclude peace, contract alliances, establish commerce, & to do all other

35   acts and things which independant states may of right do. And for the

36   support of this declaration we mutually pledge to each other our lives, our

37   fortunes, & our sacred honour.

On the morning of Friday, June 28, it was business as usual in the Continental Congress. In carriages, on horseback, and afoot, delegates entered the State House from Chestnut Street while behind the big building, on Walnut Street, British soldiers and American collaborators languished in the iron-barred rooms of the new jail, sprawling against the cool stone walls out of the sun. The redcoats wondered if they would be released in exchange for the Americans freed at Cedars.

Inside the State House, in the white-paneled meeting room, seated at their tables in their high-backed cushioned chairs, the delegates heard a report of the Committee of Claims, and agreed to pay Thomas Thomson

> 750 Dollars, in part of an account for Lumber said to
> have been delivered by Simon Metcalf to the forces be-
> longing to the Continent at St. Johns in Canada;

and to pay Thomas Mayberry 117 29/90 dollars for plated iron. The dollar, divided into 90 parts, was just coming into use as the currency of Congress, in place of the British pound.

After two petitions had been referred to committees, the next order of business was the presentation of the credentials of five new New Jersey delegates who had been elected by the state's new provincial (rebel) assembly on June 21.

Now it was time for Jefferson to present his draft of the Declaration. He read it aloud while the delegates huddled over their tables shuffling papers and writing, hardly listening to his words, conferring with each other behind cupped hands or wandering out of the hall for some refreshment. There was no way of telling what they thought of the paper. Dr. Franklin, back in Congress for the first time since June 11, had listened attentively. Jefferson was pleased that the old man was back, to join Adams in his support.

President Hancock directed that the Declaration be tabled until the matter of independence itself—the vote on Richard Henry Lee's resolution—had been decided. It was scheduled for Monday, July 1, the end of the three-week waiting period that had commenced on June 10.

It was becoming quite hot, and many delegates were fanning themselves. But there was more business before they could adjourn: petitions, new committees to be formed, more resolutions, a million dollars in additional funds to be printed and issued.

Jefferson would have to wait for the final assault on his work.

Left, overleaf: *The first page of the copy of the Declaration that Jefferson made for his friend George Wythe; a very close approximation of the form in which the document was presented to Congress on June 28.* (New York Public Library)

Right, overleaf: *Type reconstruction. Jefferson made at least five copies of the Declaration early in July. Brackets showed passages deleted by Congress, otherwise they were neat copies of the final stage of the Rough Draft.*

A Declaration by the Representatives of the UNITED STATES OF
AMERICA in General Congress assembled.

When in the course of human events it becomes necessary for one people to
dissolve the political bands which have connected them with another, and to assume
among the powers of the earth the separate and equal station to which the laws of na-
-ture & of nature's god entitle them, a decent respect to the opinions of mankind re-
-quires that they should declare the causes which impel them to the separation.

We hold these truths to be self evident; that all men are created equal; that
they are endowed by their Creator with inherent & inalienable rights; that among
these are life, liberty, & the pursuit of happiness; that to secure these rights, govern-
-ments are instituted among men, deriving their just powers from the consent of the
governed; that whenever any form of government becomes destructive of these ends,
it is the right of the people to alter or to abolish it, and to institute new government,
laying it's foundation on such principles & organising it's powers in such form as to
them shall seem most likely to effect their safety & happiness. prudence indeed will
dictate that governments long established should not be changed for light & transient
causes. and accordingly all experience hath shewn that mankind are more disposed to
suffer while evils are sufferable, ~~~~~~~~~~~, themselves by abolishing the forms
they are accustomed. but when a long train of abuses & usurpations, begun at a distin-
-guished period, & pursuing invariably the same object, evinces a design to reduce them
under absolute despotism, it is their right, it is their duty, to throw off such government
& to provide new guards for their future security. such has been the patient sufferance
of these colonies; & such is now the necessity which constrains them to expunge their
former systems of government. the history of the present king of Great Britain, is a
history of unremitting injuries & usurpations, among which appears no solitary fact
to contradict the uniform~ nor of the rest; but all have in direct object the esta-
-blishment of an absolute tyranny over these states. to prove this let facts be sub-
-mitted to a candid world, for the truth of which we pledge a faith yet unsullied by falsehood
He has refused his assent to laws the most wholesome & necessary for the public good:
he has forbidden his governors to pass laws of immediate & pressing importance, un-
-less suspended in their operation till his assent should be obtained; & when so
suspended, he has neglected utterly to attend to them.
he has refused to pass other laws for the accomodation of large districts of people, unless
those people would relinquish the right of representation in the legislature,
a right inestimable to them & formidable to tyrants only:

A Declaration by the Representatives of the
UNITED STATES OF AMERICA *in General Congress assembled*

When in the course of human events it becomes necessary for one people to dissolve the political bands which have connected them with another, and to assume among the powers of the earth the separate and equal station to which the laws of na--ture & of nature's god entitle them, a decent respect to the opinions of mankind re--quires that they should declare the causes which impel them to the separation.

We hold these truths to be self evident; that all men are created equal; that they are endowed by their Creator with inherent & inalienable rights; that among these are life, liberty, & the pursuit of happiness; that to secure these rights, govern--ments are instituted among men, deriving their just powers from the consent of the governed; that whenever any form of government becomes destructive of these ends, it is the right of the people to alter or to abolish it, and to institute new government, laying it's foundation on such principles & organising it's powers in such form, as to them shall seem most likely to effect their safety & happiness. prudence indeed will dictate that governments long established should not be changed for light & transient causes; and accordingly all experience hath shewn that mankind are more disposed to suffer while evils are sufferable than to right themselves by abolishing the forms to which they are accustomed. but when a long train of abuses and usurpations, begun at a distin--guished period & pursuing invariably the same object, evinces a design to reduce them under absolute despotism, it is their right, it is their duty, to throw off such government, & to provide new guards for their future security. such has been the patient sufferance of these colonies; & such is now the necessity which constrains them to expunge their former systems of government. the history of the present king of Great Britain is a history of unremitting injuries & usurpations, among which appears no solitary fact to contradict the uniform tenor of the rest; but all have in direct object the esta--blishment of an absolute tyranny over these states. to prove this let facts be sub--mitted to a candid world, for the truth of which we pledge a faith yet unsullied by falsehood. He has refused his assent to laws the most wholesome and necessary for the public good. he has forbidden his governors to pass laws of immediate & pressing importance, un--less suspended in their operation till his assent should be obtained; & when so suspended, he has neglected utterly to attend to them. he has refused to pass other laws for the accomodation of large districts of people, unless those people would relinquish the right of representation in the legislature, a right inestimable to them and formidable to tyrants only;

Many artists sought to reconstruct the moment when American independence was born. They had to track down the participants years after the event. As Robert Edge Pine, who made the painting from which this engraving was copied, visited, and possibly even sketched inside, the Pennsylvania State House, between 1784 and 1788, this is the most accurate rendering we have of the actual appearance of the room in which the great event took place. When Pine died in 1788, the unfinished work was purchased by Edward Savage, who added some figures, but still had not gotten around to completing it by the time of his death, in 1818. This is a copper engraving that Savage made from his and Pine's painting. Jefferson is shown handing the Declaration to Hancock. The man writing at the table to Hancock's right is Francis Hopkinson of New Jersey. Secretary Thomson is seated to the left of Hancock (as we view the picture). Others who have been identified are Charles Carroll of Maryland (in the chair at the right), talking to Stephen Hopkins of Rhode Island (in the hat). George Read of Delaware stands between them, pointing to a piece of paper. The two men seated in the left foreground are Samuel Adams (Massachusetts) and, with the stick, Robert Morris (Pennsylvania). Seated behind Samuel Adams is Robert Treat Payne (Massachusetts). Standing behind Morris are Dr. Benjamin Rush (Pennsylvania) and William Paca (Maryland). The man seated in the background to Paca's right is James Wilson (Pennsylvania). One mystery about the picture is the identity of the man standing in the center with his back to Jefferson. Presumably the central figures are intended to be the five members of the committee that prepared the Declaration. The man with his hand tucked under his waistcoat is clearly John Adams. Roger Sherman stands to Adams's right, and Franklin is seated to Jefferson's right. The fifth member of the committee was Robert R. Livingston, but the man with his back to Jefferson looks nothing like him. The best guess is that it is William Ellery (Rhode Island). (The Rhode Islander is the only delegate other than Wilson who is habitually depicted as wearing eyeglasses.) But if it is Ellery, why did Pine put him in such a prominent place?

(Library of Congress)

he has called together legislative bodies at places unusual, uncomfortable, & distant

from the depository of their public records, for the sole purpose of fatiguing them

into compliance with his measures:

he has dissolved Representative houses repeatedly & continually for opposing with

manly firmness his invasions on the rights of the people;

he has refused for a long time after such dissolutions to cause others to be elected, where-

-by the legislative powers, incapable of annihilation, have returned to the people

at large for their exercise, the state remaining in the mean time exposed to all the

dangers of invasion from without & convulsions within:

he has endeavored to prevent the population of these states; for that purpose obstructing

the laws for naturalisation of foreigners, refusing to pass others to encourage their

migrations hither; & raising the conditions of new appropriations of lands;

he has suffered the administration of justice totally to cease in some of these states, refusing

his assent to laws for establishing judiciary powers:

he has made our judges dependant on his will alone, for the tenure of their offices & the

amount and paiment of their salaries:

he has erected a multitude of new offices by a self-assumed power & sent hither swarms of

new officers to harrass our people & eat out their substance:

he has kept among us in times of peace standing armies & ships of war, without the con-

-sent of our legislatures:

he has affected to render the military independant of, and superior to, the civil power:

he has combined with others to subject us to a jurisdiction foreign to our constitutions, and

unacknoleged by our laws; giving his assent to their acts of pretended legislation

for quartering large bodies of armed troops among us;

for protecting them by a mock-trial from punishment for any murders which they

shall commit on the inhabitants of these states;

for cutting off our trade with all parts of the world;

for imposing taxes on us without our consent;

for depriving us of the benefits of trial by jury;

for transporting us beyond seas to be tried for pretended offences;

for abolishing the free system of English laws in a neighboring province, establish-

-ing therein an arbitrary government, and enlarging it's boundaries, so as to

render it at once an example & fit instrument for introducing the same abso-

-lute rule into these states;

for taking away our charters, abolishing our most valuable laws, and altering fundamentally the forms of our governments:

for suspending our own legislatures & declaring themselves invested with power
to legislate for us in all cases whatsoever:

he has abdicated government here, withdrawing his governors, & declaring us out of
his allegiance & protection:

he has plundered our seas, ravaged our coasts, burnt our towns, & destroyed the lives of our people:

he is at this time transporting large armies of foreign mercenaries to compleat the works
of death, desolation & tyranny, already begun with circumstances of cruelty & per-
-fidy unworthy the head of a civilised nation:

he has endeavored to bring on the inhabitants of our frontiers the merciless Indian
savages, whose known rule of warfare is an undistinguished destruction of all
ages, sexes, & conditions of existence:

he has incited treasonable insurrections of our fellow-citizens with the allurements
of forfeiture & confiscation of our property:

he has constrained others, taken captive on the high seas, to bear arms against their
country, to become the executioners of their friends and brethren, or to fall
themselves by their hands:

he has waged cruel war against human nature itself violating it's most sacred rights
of life & liberty in the persons of a distant people who never offended him, capti-
-vating & carrying them into slavery in another hemisphere or to incur miserable
death in their transportation thither. this piratical warfare, the opprobrium
of infidel powers, is the warfare of the Christian king of Great Britain deter-
-mined to keep open a market where MEN should be bought & sold, he has
prostituted his negative for suppressing every legislative attempt to prohibit
or to restrain this execrable commerce; and that this assemblage of horrors
might want no fact of distinguished dye, he is now exciting these very people to
rise in arms among us, and to purchase that liberty of which he has deprived them
by murdering the people upon whom he also obtruded them; thus paying off former crimes
committed against the liberties of one people with crimes which he urges them
to commit against the lives of another.

in every stage of these oppressions we have petitioned for redress in the most humble terms; our
repeated petitions have been answered only by repeated injury. a prince whose character is
thus marked by every act which may define a tyrant, is unfit to be the ruler of a people who
mean to be free. future ages will scarce believe that the hardiness of one man adventured
within the short compass of twelve years only, to build a foundation so broad & undisguised
for tyranny over a people fostered & fixed in principles of freedom.

Reconstruction of the third page of the Declaration, based on the Wythe copy, as Jefferson presented it to Congress.

Right: *Reconstruction of the fourth page of the Declaration, based on the Wythe copy and the Rough Draft, as Jefferson presented it to Congress.*

One reason it is thought that Jefferson made this copy on the evening of July 3 is the bracketing of the words Scotch *and* in the middle *of the first paragraph. Since Jefferson has bracketed those two words and not anything else in the paragraph, it would seem that he made this copy after Congress had criticized that expression, but before it had decided to cut most of the paragraph. Since Congress started going over the document on the afternoon of July 2, it is doubtful that it could have reached the last page before July 3. It seems likely, then, that Jefferson bracketed* Scotch *and* on July 3 and made this copy for George Wythe that night, before most of the remaining paragraph was cut. He also, for some reason, reverted to the American spelling of* honor *(last line). Jefferson made two minor slips in copying this page for Wythe. On the sixth line from the bottom, he put* parliament or people *instead of* people or parliament *(see Rough Draft, page 90). And on the next line he left out* and declare *in* assert and declare. *Perhaps it was late in the evening, and the light was failing, or he was weary.*

Nor have we been wanting in attentions to our British brethren. we have warned them from time to time of attempts by their legislature to extend a jurisdiction over these our states. we have reminded them of the circumstances of our emigration & settlement here, no one of which could warrant so strange a pretension: that these were effected at the expence of our own blood & treasure, unassisted by the wealth or the strength of Great Britain: that in constituting indeed our several forms of government, we had a--dopted one common king, thereby laying a foundation for perpetual league & amity with them: but that submission to their parliament was no part of our constitution, nor ever in idea, if history may be credited: and we appealed to their native justice & magnanimity, as well as to the ties of our common kindred, to disavow these usur--pations, which were likely to interrupt our connection & correspondence. they too have been deaf to the voice of justice & of consanguinity and when occasions have been given them by the regular course of their laws, of removing from their councils the disturbers of our harmony, they have by their free election re-established them in power. at this very time too, they are permitting their chief magistrate to send over not only soldiers of our common blood, but [Scotch and] foreign mercenaries to invade & destroy us. these facts have given the last stab to agonizing affection, and manly spirit bids us to renounce for ever these unfeeling brethren. we must endeavor to forget our former love for them, and to hold them, as we hold the rest of mankind, enemies in war, in peace friends. we might have been a free & a great people together; but a communication of grandeur and of freedom, it seems, is below their dignity. be it so, since they will have it. the road to happiness & to glory is open to us too: we will climb it apart from them, and ac--quiesce in the necessity which denounces our eternal separation!

We therefore the Representatives of the United States of America, in General Congress assembled, do, in the name & by the authority of the good people of these states, reject and renounce all allegiance & subjection to the kings of Great Britain, and all others who may hereafter claim by, through or under them; we utterly dissolve all political connection which may heretofore have subsisted between us & the parliament or people of Great Britain; and finally we do assert these colonies to be free & independent states, and that as free & independant states, they have full power to levy war, conclude peace, contract alliances, establish commerce, & do all other acts and things which inde--pendant states may of right do. And for the support of this declaration, we mu--tually pledge to each other our lives, our fortunes & our sacred honor.

CHAPTER TWELVE

Independence

On the evening of Saturday, June 29, Jefferson dined at Smith's Tavern. He also paid 39 shillings 9 pence for laundry (the dollar was not yet accepted as currency in Philadelphia), and bought a pencil and map from the merchant Sparhawk. On Sunday, the 30th, he went riding in the country to the place where his other two horses were pastured, and wrote a letter. He had just received word of his reelection to Congress. He wanted President Pendleton of the Virginia assembly to know that, despite this, he expected to be allowed to go home by August 10, the expiration of his present term.

There was still resistance to independence in South Carolina and some of the Middle states, but the tide was unmistakably running in the other direction. New delegates instructed for independence had already arrived from New Jersey. Other new provincial assemblies were meeting in New York and Maryland, and the Pennsylvania assembly was gathered that very Sunday in Carpenters Hall in Philadelphia. One of its tasks was to try to change the vote on independence. With Dickinson, Robert Morris, and James Wilson on the side of delay, and Franklin and John Morton (whose shift to independence had begun with Samuel Adams's speech three weeks before) on the side of independence, Pennsylvania's vote in Congress was still 3 to 2 for delay. The new Pennsylvania assembly was unable to elect a new delegation.

Early Monday morning, Jefferson, as a member of a new committee inquiring into "the miscarriages [defeats and failures] in Canada," took the testimony of a Montreal merchant, John Blake.

It was a hot and humid day. As Jefferson and Bob Hemings rode from the tavern where Blake was staying, to the State House, they passed weeds flourishing along the edges of vacant lots, and swarms of white butterflies hovering over piles of horse manure.

One of the blank pages in Timothy Telescope's Almanak *that Jefferson used for keeping his 1776 accounts. This page runs from June 20 to July 6. It appears that Jefferson forgot that June had only thirty days. This error must have had its origin in his writing "30" in place of "29." June 30 was a Sunday, and he could hardly have purchased a pencil and a map at Sparhawk's on the Sabbath. On the other hand, he often went riding on Sundays, so that "31" must refer to the thirtieth. Notice the reference to "Bob" on June 25.* (Massachusetts Historical Society)

Edward Rutledge, twenty-six, was the youngest member of Congress. John Adams at first scorned him as "a peacock, excessively vain . . . weak . . . unsteady . . . inane and puerile." But by June 1776, he had more experience in Congress than any other member of the South Carolina delegation, and led it into finally voting for independence. (Museum of Early Southern Decorative Arts, Winston-Salem, North Carolina)

Delegates were still drifting into the State House. Congress was beginning its deliberations at nine o'clock, one hour earlier than usual. President Hancock read from the eighteen letters that had accumulated since Friday. Three, sent by General Washington, enclosed a number of papers, including a *General Return of the Army of the* UNITED COLONIES showing that of the 10,368 rank and file under his command, 7,389 were present and fit for duty. In his letters, the Commander-in-Chief defended the efficiency of Commissary-General Trumbull, requested new regulations covering chaplains, and told of a plot that had been uncovered. The soldier Thomas Hickey had been sentenced to death for planning to assassinate staff officers and blow up powder magazines as the King's troops arrived in New York.

Three hours passed. It was noon when Congress was at last ready, now that the three-week waiting period was over, to take up the Lee resolution on independence. John Hancock stepped down from the raised platform and Benjamin Harrison took his place. The Continental Congress had once more become a Committee of the Whole.

The arguments for and against independence had been heard so many times that it was expected that little more would be said. However, John Dickinson arose in his elegant plum-colored suit, armed with pamphlets and newspaper clippings, to again explain his position. He argued that the colonies ought to form a government and make a French alliance *before* taking the dangerous step of separation. In the present circumstances, without even a single military victory, they would be fools to launch themselves with a mere declaration, a "skiff made of paper."

John Adams waited for someone to make a reply, but the eloquent among his allies were absent. Richard Henry Lee had returned to Virginia, Christopher Gadsden to South Carolina, and John Sullivan of New Hampshire was in the army. Still Adams waited, hoping that "someone less obnoxious than [him]self, who had been all along for a Year before, and was still . . . believed to be the Author of all the Mischief," would get up.

Realizing, finally, that if he did not answer Dickinson no one would, Adams made what was reported to be one of the best speeches of his career, accented with thumps of his hickory stick on the floor. Just as he was finishing, and resuming his seat, the new five-man delegation from New Jersey returned. They requested that Adams repeat his arguments for them. Adams later wrote:

> All was Silence: No one would speak: all Eyes were turned upon me. Mr. Edward Rutledge came to me and said laughing, "Nobody will speak but you, upon this Subject. You have all the Topicks so ready, that you must satisfy the gentlemen from New Jersey." I answered him laughing, that it had so much the Air of exhibiting, like an Actor or Gladiator for the Entertainment of the Audience, that I was ashamed to repeat what I had said twenty times before, and thought nothing new could be advanced by me.

But he did go through it again.

Then came the vote. Nine colonies were in favor: New Hampshire, Vermont, Connecticut, Massachusetts, New Jersey, Maryland, Virginia, North Carolina, and Georgia. South Carolina and Pennsylvania were opposed; Delaware, with only two of its three members present, was divided; and New York, still waiting for new instructions from its assembly, was abstaining.

President Hancock resumed the chair and Benjamin Harrison reported the vote. The Committee of the Whole was in favor of independence by a vote of 9 to 2. Now Edward Rutledge of South Carolina got up. Three weeks before, he had requested a delay in hopes of staving off independence for a year or more. Now he asked that the recording of the tally be put off a day in hopes of unanimity for

The part of the British fleet that had sailed down from Halifax, Nova Scotia, after leaving Boston, as it appeared off Staten Island. The far shore is Brooklyn. The sketch was made by Captain Archibald Robertson, Royal Engineers, on July 12, 1776. (The New York Public Library, Spencer Collection)

independence. There were more resolutions, another letter from General Washington, and Congress adjourned until ten the following morning.

The delegates had some interesting and alarming news to digest along with dinner. Sir William Howe's fleet of British warships, which General Washington had driven out of Boston in March, had been sighted off Sandy Hook, New Jersey, more than sixty sail headed for New York Harbor.

Tuesday morning, July 2, Jefferson, for the Committee of Inquiry into the Miscarriages in Canada, took more testimony from two other witnesses. He interviewed Captain Hector McNeal, a former resident of Quebec, and Dr. Coates, who had accompanied General Arnold from Cambridge. It was cloudy, and by the time the delegates entered the State House, a heavy rain was falling.

After the reading of just five letters, Congress turned itself back into a Committee of the Whole. South Carolina changed its votes, with Edward Rutledge announcing that his state now favored independence. The third Delaware delegate, Caesar Rodney, arrived after an all-night ride through thunderstorms to put his state on the side of independence. Pennsylvania was also able to change its vote because Robert Morris and John Dickinson agreed to stay away. (Dickinson was home packing, preparing to accompany his troop of Pennsylvania volunteers to New York where they would join General Washington's forces.) With these two opponents of immediate independence absent, and with James Wilson switching his vote, Pennsylvania came out for separation. New York was still forced to abstain, but the vote was 12 to 0 for independence.

To the members of Congress, the Lee resolution

> Resolved that these United Colonies are, and of right
> ought to be, free and independent States

was the declaration of independence. Jefferson's Declaration, which would soon be taken up in a Committee of the Whole, was seen important as propaganda, but the Lee resolution was independence itself. Its passage by a 12 to 0 vote made the colonies independent. So, naturally, the Continental Congress expected that this would be the day remembered in history. John Adams wrote his wife that

> The second day of July, 1776, will be the most memorable epocha in the history of America. . . . It will be celebrated by succeeding generations as the great anniversary festival . . .

On that same day General Sir William Howe landed 10,000 British regulars on Staten Island, less than a hundred miles from Philadelphia.

CHAPTER THIRTEEN

Sixty Editors

Now, in the middle of Tuesday afternoon, July 2, 1776, as the rain stopped and the skies cleared, began Thomas Jefferson's ordeal. Congress went over his Declaration paragraph by paragraph. The process took about twelve hours: Tuesday afternoon, most of Wednesday, and several hours on Thursday.

A great many changes in wording were made, and some extensive cuts. The third page underwent major surgery. Half of it was eliminated, including the long slavery charge. The Georgia and South Carolina delegations attacked it, while John Adams defended it.

Unlike Virginia, Georgia and South Carolina had never sought to end the slave trade. They could hardly sign a document blaming the King for continuing a trade that they desired, without feeling like hypocrites. Nor did all the Northern states wish to condemn slavery. As Jefferson noted, "tho' their people have very few slaves themselves yet they had been pretty considerable carriers of them for others."

Right: Reconstruction of the first page of the Declaration showing Congress's changes.

Congress made few changes on the all-important first page. According to all reports, Jefferson, at the time, didn't like any of them.

A Declaration by the Representatives of the
UNITED STATES OF AMERICA *in General Congress assembled*

1   When in the course of human events it becomes necessary for one people to

2   dissolve the political bands which have connected them with another, and to assume

3   among the powers of the earth the separate and equal station to which the laws of na-

4   -ture & of nature's god entitle them, a decent respect to the opinions of mankind re-

5   -quires that they should declare the causes which impel them to the separation.

6   We hold these truths to be self evident; that all men are created equal; that

7   they are endowed by their Creator with ~~inherent &~~ *certain* inalienable rights; that among

8   these are life, liberty, & the pursuit of happiness; that to secure these rights, govern-

9   -ments are instituted among men, deriving their just powers from the consent of the

10   governed; that whenever any form of government becomes destructive of these ends,

11   it is the right of the people to alter or to abolish it, and to institute new government,

12   laying it's foundation on such principles & organising it's powers in such form, as to

13   them shall seem most likely to effect their safety & happiness. prudence indeed will

14   dictate that governments long established should not be changed for light & transient

15   causes; and accordingly all experience hath shewn that mankind are more disposed to

16   suffer while evils are sufferable than to right themselves by abolishing the forms to which

17   they are accustomed. but when a long train of abuses and usurpations, ~~begun at a distin-~~

18   ~~-guished period &~~ pursuing invariably the same object, evinces a design to reduce them

19   under absolute despotism, it is their right, it is their duty, to throw off such government,

20   & to provide new guards for their future security. such has been the patient sufferance

21   of these colonies; & such is now the necessity which constrains them to ~~expunge~~ *alter* their

22   former systems of government. the history of the present king of Great Britain is a

23   history of ~~unremitting~~ *repeated* injuries & usurpations, ~~among which appears no solitary fact~~

24   ~~to contradict the uniform tenor of the rest; but all have~~ *all having* in direct object the esta-

25   -blishment of an absolute tyranny over these states. to prove this let facts be sub-

26   -mitted to a candid world, ~~for the truth of which we pledge a faith yet unsullied by falsehood.~~

27   He has refused his assent to laws the most wholesome and necessary for the public good.

28   he has forbidden his governors to pass laws of immediate & pressing importance, un-

29   -less suspended in their operation till his assent should be obtained; & when so

30   suspended, he has ^*utterly* neglected ~~utterly~~ to attend to them.

31   he has refused to pass other laws for the accomodation of large districts of people, unless

32   those people would relinquish the right of representation in the legislature,

33   a right inestimable to them and formidable to tyrants only;

Artist John Trumbull's version of the presentation of the Declaration. The ages of the committee members are shown more accurately than in the Pine and Savage work, but the chairs are the wrong style. Trumbull traveled all over the United States and abroad, seeking out living signers of the Declaration, or good likenesses of those who had died, and painting their heads on small mahogany panels—his visual "notes" for the large canvas that he worked on from 1786 until 1818. Although the scene purports to be June 28, 1776, some delegates who were present then are omitted and others, who were not present,

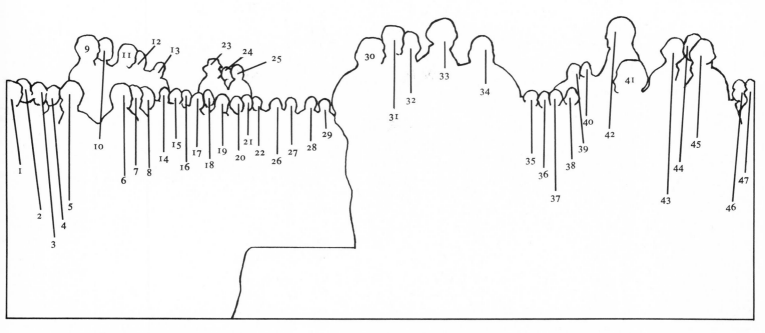

1. George Wythe, Virginia
2. William Whipple, New Hampshire
3. Josiah Bartlett, New Hampshire
4. Benjamin Harrison, Virginia
5. Thomas Lynch, South Carolina
6. Richard Henry Lee, Virginia
7. Samuel Adams, Massachusetts
8. George Clinton, New York
9. William Paca, Maryland
10. Samuel Chase, Maryland
11. Lewis Morris, New York
12. William Floyd, New York
13. Arthur Middleton, Connecticut
14. Thomas Heyward, South Carolina
15. Charles Carroll, Maryland
16. George Walton, Georgia
17. Robert Morris, Pennsylvania
18. Thomas Willing, Pennsylvania
19. Benjamin Rush, Pennsylvania
20. Elbridge Gerry, Massachusetts
21. Robert Treat Payne, Massachusetts
22. Abraham Clark, New Jersey
23. Stephen Hopkins, Rhode Island
24. William Ellery, Rhode Island

25. George Clymer, Pennsylvania
26. William Hooper, North Carolina
27. Joseph Hewes, North Carolina
28. James Wilson, Pennsylvania
29. Francis Hopkinson, New Jersey
30. John Adams, Massachusetts
31. Roger Sherman, Connecticut
32. Robert R. Livingston, New York
33. Thomas Jefferson, Virginia
34. Benjamin Franklin, Pennsylvania
35. Richard Stockton, New Jersey
36. Francis Lewis, New York
37. John Witherspoon, New Jersey
38. Samuel Huntington, Connecticut
39. William Williams, Connecticut
40. Oliver Wolcott, Connecticut
41. John Hancock, Massachusetts
42. Charles Thomson, Pennsylvania
43. George Read, Delaware
44. John Dickinson, Pennsylvania
45. Edward Rutledge, South Carolina
46. Thomas McKean, Pennsylvania
47. Philip Livingston, New York

but who signed the document on August 2, are shown. Of the forty-seven persons depicted, thirty-six were painted from life, nine from portraits by other painters, and two (William Whipple and Benjamin Harrison) were reconstructed from memory. A number of delegates were left out simply because Trumbull could find no satisfactory portraits of them. John Dickinson of Pennsylvania, the man who rewrote Jefferson's 1775 Declaration, is shown in the center of the group of three men standing at the right. (Library of Congress)

Right: *Reconstruction of the second page of the Declaration showing Congress's changes.*

It was more accurate to say that the King had injured colonies *than* states *(next-to-last line).*

1   he has called together legislative bodies at places unusual, uncomfortable, & distant

2   from the depository of their public records, for the sole purpose of fatiguing them

3   into compliance with his measures:

4   he has dissolved Representative houses repeatedly ~~& continually~~ for opposing with

5   manly firmness his invasions on the rights of the people;

6   he has refused for a long time after such dissolutions to cause others to be elected, where-

7   -by the legislative powers, incapable of annihilation, have returned to the people

8   at large for their exercise, the state remaining in the mean time exposed to all the

9   dangers of invasion from without & convulsions within:

10 he has endeavored to prevent the population of these states; for that purpose obstructing

11   the laws for naturalisation of foreigners, refusing to pass others to encourage their

12   migrations hither; & raising the conditions of new appropriations of lands;

13 he has ~~suffered~~ *obstructed* the administration of justice ~~totally to cease in some of these states,~~ *by* refusing

14   his assent to laws for establishing judiciary powers:

15 he has made ~~our~~ judges dependant on his will alone, for the tenure of their offices & the

16   amount and paiment of their salaries:

17 he has erected a multitude of new offices ~~by a self-assumed power~~ & sent hither swarms of

18   new officers to harrass our people & eat out their substance:

19 he has kept among us in times of peace standing armies ~~& ships of war,~~ without the con-

20   -sent of our legislatures:

21 he has affected to render the military independant of, and superior to, the civil power:

22 he has combined with others to subject us to a jurisdiction foreign to our constitutions, and

23   unacknoleged by our laws; giving his assent to their acts of pretended legislation

24   for quartering large bodies of armed troops among us;

25   for protecting them by a mock-trial from punishment for any murders which they

26   should commit on the inhabitants of these states;

27   for cutting off our trade with all parts of the world;

28   for imposing taxes on us without our consent;

29   for depriving us *in many cases* of the benefits of trial by jury;

30   for transporting us beyond seas to be tried for pretended offences;

31   for abolishing the free system of English laws in a neighboring province, establish-

32   -ing therein an arbitrary government, and enlarging it's boundaries, so as to

33   render it at once an example & fit instrument for introducing the same abso-

34   -lute rule into these ~~states~~ *colonies*;

35 for taking away our charters, abolishing our most valuable laws, and altering

Right: *Reconstruction of the third page of the Declaration showing Congress's changes.*

This was the scene of Jefferson's greatest defeat. He needed the slavery passage to be comfortable with himself as owner of 187 slaves. And just as he needed to assure himself that slavery would be ended by his descendants, so he wanted the Declaration itself to promise that slavery would not endure in the United States of America.

Not even John Adams had approved of the personal attack on King George III (last five lines).

There seems also to have been a suggestion, in Congress, to move the reference to the Scotch to the charge on transporting armies (See Rough Draft, line 8, page 86).

1   fundamentally the forms of our governments:

2   for suspending our own legislatures & declaring themselves invested with power

3   to legislate for us in all cases whatsoever:

by declaring us out of his protection & waging war against us

4   he has abdicated government here, ~~withdrawing his governors, & declaring us out of~~

5   ~~his allegiance & protection:~~

6   he has plundered our seas, ravaged our coasts, burnt our towns, & destroyed the lives of our people:

7   he is at this time transporting large armies of foreign mercenaries to compleat the works

8   of death, desolation & tyranny, already begun with circumstances of cruelty & per-

scarcely paralleled in the most barbarous ages and totally

9   -fidy ∧ unworthy the head of a civilised nation:

excited domestic insurrections amongst us and has

10   he has ∧ endeavored to bring on the inhabitants of our frontiers the merciless Indian

11   savages, whose known rule of warfare is an undistinguished destruction of all

12   ages, sexes, & conditions ~~of existence:~~

13   ~~he has incited treasonable insurrections of our fellow-citizens with the allurements~~

14   ~~of forfeiture & confiscation of our property:~~

15   he has constrained others, taken captive on the high seas, to bear arms against their

16   country, to become the executioners of their friends and brethren, or to fall

17   themselves by their hands:

18   ~~he has waged cruel war against human nature itself violating it's most sacred rights~~

19   ~~of life & liberty in the persons of a distant people who never offended him, capti-~~

20   ~~-vating & carrying them into slavery in another hemisphere or to incur miserable~~

21   ~~death in their transportation thither. this piratical warfare, the opprobrium~~

22   ~~of infidel powers, is the warfare of the Christian king of Great Britain deter-~~

23   ~~-mined to keep open a market where MEN should be bought & sold, he has~~

24   ~~prostituted his negative for suppressing every legislative attempt to prohibit~~

25   ~~or to restrain this execrable commerce; and that this assemblage of horrors~~

26   ~~might want no fact of distinguished dye, he is now exciting these very people to~~

27   ~~rise in arms among us, and to purchase that liberty of which he has deprived them~~

28   ~~by murdering the people upon whom he also obtruded them; thus paying off former crimes~~

29   ~~committed against the liberties of one people with crimes which he urges them~~

30   ~~to commit against the lives of another.~~

31   in every stage of these oppressions we have petitioned for redress in the most humble terms; our

32   repeated petitions have been answered only by repeated injury. a prince whose character is

free

33   thus marked by every act which may define a tyrant, is unfit to be the ruler of a ∧ people ~~who~~

34   ~~mean to be free. future ages will scarce believe that the hardiness of one man adventured~~

35   ~~within the short compass of twelve years only, to build a foundation so broad & undisguised~~

36   ~~for tyranny over a people fostered & fixed in principles of freedom.~~

It may have been after the slavery passage had been removed—perhaps late in the afternoon of July 3—that Franklin, sitting beside Jefferson, leaned over to comfort him with a famous story:

"I have made it a rule, whenever in my power," Franklin whispered, "to avoid becoming the draughtsman of papers to be reviewed by a public body. I took my lesson from an incident I will relate to you. When I was a journeyman printer, one of my companions, an apprentice Hatter, having served out his time, was about to open shop for himself. His first concern was to have a handsome signboard with a proper inscription. He composed it in these words:

JOHN THOMPSON, HATTER, MAKES AND SELLS HATS
FOR READY MONEY

with a figure of a hat subjoined. But he thought he would submit it to his friends for their amendments.

"The first he shewed it to thought the word *hatter* tautologous, because followed by the words, *makes hats* which shew he was a hatter. It was struck out. The next observed that the word *makes* might just as well be omitted, because his customers would not care who makes the hats. If good and to their mind, they would buy, by whomsoever made. He struck it out. A third said he thought the words *for ready money* were useless as it was not the custom of the place to sell on credit. Everyone who purchased expected to pay. They were parted with, and the inscription now stood

JOHN THOMPSON SELLS HATS.

" 'Sells hats' says his next friend. 'Why nobody will expect you to give them away. What is the use of that word?' It was stricken out, and *hats* followed it, the rather, as there was one painted on the board. So his inscription was reduced ultimately to

JOHN THOMPSON

with the figure of a hat subjoined."

On Wednesday evening, after his ordeal in Congress, Jefferson consoled himself by purchasing a Fahrenheit thermometer from Sparhawk for 3 pounds 15 shillings, an extravagant sum, more than a month's wages for a laborer.

The following morning, at six o'clock, an hour after rising, Jefferson noted that the temperature outside was 68°F and that the wind was coming from the southeast from the mosquito-infested swamps and odorous Dock Creek. Having soaked his feet in the daily basin of cold water fetched by his young valet, he sipped his tea, nibbled some wafers, and went to call on General David Wooster in connection with his work for the committee inquiring into the miscarriages in Canada. Jefferson took some three pages of testimony, much of which concerned the manner in which the small-pox had weakened the army. What with taking Wooster's testimony, and recording the day's temperature again at nine o'clock (it had warmed up to 72¼°F), Jefferson arrived at the State House after the day's meeting was scheduled to start.

The fourth of July was even worse for Jefferson than the third. The rest of the Declaration (all of the fourth page, we are assuming) remained to be edited. Congress, after dispensing with two resolutions and asking the Pennsylvania Committee of Safety to send flints to the army in New York, proceeded to slash away at Jefferson's draft.

One delegate quibbled that roads were *trod*, not *climbed*, but what made the most trouble for Jefferson on the fourth page was his reference to *Scotch & other foreign mercenaries*. John Witherspoon, James Wilson, Thomas McKean and other delegates of Scotch descent were annoyed at being classed with foreigners. Their anger extended to other parts of the passage as well. Some delegates thought it unwise to condemn the entire British people, many of whom were sympathetic to the colonists. Others did not think it wise to say that Parliament had no right to rule the colonies when, just a year before, Congress had admitted that Parliament did have some power over them. As a result of these different currents of criticism, all mention of Parliament was eliminated and other extensive cuts were made. Congress also added two references to God.

One can imagine Jefferson's feelings when the portion of the next-to-last paragraph on which he had spent so much time was left out.

To add insult to injury, the actual declaration (announcement) of independence, which Jefferson thought he had improved, was removed and the wording of Richard Henry Lee's resolution was put in its place.

1   Nor have we been wanting in attentions to our British brethren. we have warned

an unwarranted

2   them from time to time of attempts by their legislature to extend a jurisdiction over ~~these~~

us

3   ~~our states.~~ we have reminded them of the circumstances of our emigration & settlement

4   here, ~~no one of which could warrant so strange a pretension: that these were effected~~

5   ~~at the expence of our own blood & treasure, unassisted by the wealth or the strength of~~

6   ~~Great Britain: that in constituting indeed our several forms of government, we had a-~~

7   ~~-dopted one common king, thereby laying a foundation for perpetual league & amity~~

8   ~~with them: but that submission to their parliament was no part of our constitution, nor~~

have

9   ~~ever in idea, if history may be credited:~~ and we appealed to their native justice &

and we have conjured them by

10   magnanimity, ~~as well as to~~ the ties of our common kindred, to disavow these usur-

would inevitably

11   -pations, which ~~were likely to~~ interrupt our connection & correspondence. they too have

we must therefore

12   been deaf to the voice of justice & of consanguinity ~~and when occasions have been given~~

13   ~~them by the regular course of their laws, of removing from their councils the disturbers of~~

14   ~~our harmony, they have by their free election re-established them in power. at this very~~

15   ~~time too, they are permitting their chief magistrate to send over not only soldiers of our~~

16   ~~common blood, but Scotch and foreign mercenaries to invade & destroy us. these facts~~

17   ~~have given the last stab to agonizing affection, and manly spirit bids us to renounce~~

18   ~~for ever these unfeeling brethren. we must endeavor to forget our former love for them,~~

19   ~~and to hold them, as we hold the rest of mankind, enemies in war, in peace friends.~~

20   ~~we might have been a free & a great people together; but a communication of grandeur~~

21   ~~and of freedom, it seems, is below their dignity. be it so, since they will have it. the road~~

22   ~~to happiness & to glory is open to us too: we will climb it apart from them, and~~ ac-

23   quiesce in the necessity which denounces our ~~eternal~~ separation\ *and hold them as we hold*

24   *the rest of mankind, enemies in war, in peace friends.*

25   We therefore the Representatives of the United States of America, in General

appealing to the supreme judge of the world for the rectitude of our intentions   *colonies, solemnly*

26   Congress assembled, do, in the name & by the authority of the good people of these ~~states, reject~~

publish & declare that these United colonies are & of right ought to be free & independent states; that they are

27   ~~and renounce all allegiance & subjection to the kings of Great Britain, and all others~~

absolved from all allegiance to the British Crown, and that

28   ~~who may hereafter claim by, through or under them; we utterly dissolve~~ all political

them   *state*

29   connection which may heretofore have subsisted between ~~us~~ & the ~~people or parliament~~

is & ought to be totally dissolved

30   of Great Britain; ~~and finally we do assert and declare these colonies to be free & independent states,~~

31   and that as free & independant states, they have full power to levy war, conclude peace,

32   contract alliances, establish commerce, & do all other acts and things which inde-

with a firm reliance on the protection of divine providence

33   -pendant states may of right do. And for the support of this declaration, we mu-

34   -tually pledge to each other our lives, our fortunes & our sacred honour.

Jefferson could not credit his critics with good motives. "The pusillanimous idea that we had friends in Britain worth keeping terms with," he wrote, was the "reason those passages which conveyed censures on the people of England were struck out, lest they should give them offense."

History has judged Congress's editing of the Declaration more kindly than did its author. For one thing, not many people are interested any longer in the final three pages because they are concerned with the details of a quarrel that no longer exists. What Congress did to the charges against the King does not really matter anymore. With regard to the first page, Jefferson was well served by Congress. Almost every congressional change improved the text.

Early in the afternoon of July 4, Congress ordered that the Declaration be printed and "authenticated," that is, overseen at the press and proofread by the committee of five. Printed copies were to be sent

> to the several Assemblies, Conventions, and Committees or Councils of Safety, and to the several Commanding officers of the Continental Troops. that it be proclaimed in each of the *United States*, and at the head of the Army.

The remainder of the afternoon of July 4 was taken up with numerous other congressional matters, including the dispatch of twenty-five pounds of powder to John Harrison of North Carolina.

Left: *Reconstruction of the fourth page of the Declaration showing Congress's changes.*

Why was Congress so hard on this page? For one thing, it didn't want to mention Parliament because it had once acknowledged that Parliament did have authority over it. To save embarrassment, it was better to pretend that its only connection with England had been through the King. The claim that the colonies had never needed England's strength (line 5) struck a false note. And what about the long passage, beginning at this very time too (line 14), that Jefferson had labored over? It didn't add any new thoughts but was merely, as Adams put it, "oratorical." The document was better without it. This is one of the very few times in history that an assembly of men has shortened a document rather than lengthened it; has generally improved it, rather than made it more diffuse.

CHAPTER FOURTEEN

Going to Press

There is no record of which of the five committee members went to the shop of John Dunlap to oversee the printing. Was it Jefferson, Adams, or that old printer and former employer of John Dunlap's uncle William, Benjamin Franklin? The printing was a rush job. As propaganda, the Declaration would be treated as a broadside (poster) printed on one side of a sheet of paper for display, with capital letters used to attract attention rather than in accordance with grammatical rules.

The rules of grammar in the eighteenth century were, in any case, not as firmly fixed as they are now. Nouns were capitalized haphazardly for emphasis. Jefferson went to the other extreme and used capital letters very sparingly—only at the beginnings of paragraphs and in the names of nations (Great Britain) or peoples (Indians). He used even fewer capital letters than we do today (leaving even *god* in lowercase). With all this, his style was closer to what came later than that of his contemporaries.

In setting the Declaration in type, Dunlap first of all put a new heading at the top:

IN CONGRESS, JULY 4, 1776.

In the body of the Declaration, Dunlap capitalized the entire first word of each paragraph and the first letter of most of the nouns. He also got rid of the ampersands (&), spelling out *and* in all cases.

He corrected a number of Jefferson's spellings:

Jefferson	*Dunlap*
it's	its
dependant	dependent
independant	independent
unacknoleged	unacknowledged
mock-trial	mock trial

John Dunlap came to Philadelphia from Ireland as a ten-year-old boy (1757), to be apprenticed to his uncle William, a former printing associate of Benjamin Franklin. When William sold his business to become a clergyman, John found himself, at twenty-one, the proprietor of a printing and bookselling business. Soon after, he started a newspaper. (Frick Art Reference Library, First Troop Philadelphia City Cavalry Collection)

Dunlap also hyphenated *Great-Britain*, in the accepted style of the day, and added the *u* in *endeavoured* to give it the English spelling, and changed Jefferson's *honour* to *honor*, giving it the American spelling.

Dunlap, either influenced by Adams or on his own, substituted the less frequently used *unalienable* for *inalienable* in *certain unalienable rights*. He altered the punctuation, sometimes for the better, and in the second-to-last line of the second-to-last paragraph, the word *Connection* became *Connections*.

Dunlap's apprentice dipped the leather roller into the greasy ink and squeaked it across the type. Paper was put into position, and the printer pulled the lever. The proof was examined, corrections were made, and the press run began, powered by the brawny arms of the apprentice.

The following morning a copy was glued into the Journal of Congress and others were dispatched to the states and to the troops in the field. The next day, Saturday, July 6, the Declaration appeared in a Philadelphia newspaper, the *Evening Post*.

There still had been no celebration. The members of Congress had little enough time for thoughts about their decision, let alone gaiety. They could think only of the fact of independence and its consequences. They made grim jokes about being hanged for treason. "Congress," a New Jersey delegate noted, might soon be "exalted on a high gallows."

On Monday, July 8, the *Pennsylvania Packet* announced, "This day, at twelve o'clock, the Declaration of Independence will be proclaimed at the State House." A small crowd of idlers, unemployed sailors, and a few others gathered around the platform in the State House yard to hear the Declaration read by Colonel John Nixon of the Philadelphia Committee of Safety. Bells were rung all day throughout the city. But the Liberty Bell, then in the State House steeple, probably was not rung. The rickety wooden steeple would have collapsed. The bell had been cast more than twenty years before, to celebrate the fiftieth anniversary of the Pennsylvania Assembly. Its strangely prophetic legend, *Proclaim liberty throughout the land and to the people thereof*, was taken from the Bible (Leviticus 25, 10). The verse referred to the Hebrew custom of leaving the land idle every half-century.

That evening the Declaration was read again on the Commons, at the head of each battalion of Associators (Philadelphia militia) and there was more celebration. John Adams described the scene to his wife:

> Three cheers rended the welkin [sky]. The battalions paraded . . . and gave us the *feu de joie* [firing of guns in token of joy], notwithstanding the scarcity of powder.

The next evening the Declaration was heard by each brigade of the army in New York, arousing, in Washington's words, "hearty assent" and "warmest approbation." As news of the Declaration spread through the city, a crowd, uncowed by the British fleet—now 130 ships strong—in the harbor, overturned a gilded lead statue of King George III. It was later melted into bullets. Everywhere, in the days that followed, boisterous mobs tore down the symbols of royal authority, whether coats of arms on public buildings or scepters and crowns on the signboards of inns.

Right: *The first printed version of the Declaration was the Dunlap broadside. Notice that the printer set the first of the items of* Pretended legislation, *beginning with* For, *as a paragraph, consistent with the other items in the list. Unalienable (line 6) was also Adams's way of spelling the word (see his copy of the first page of the Declaration, page 60). Perhaps, then, it was Adams who superintended the printing.* (Library of Congress)

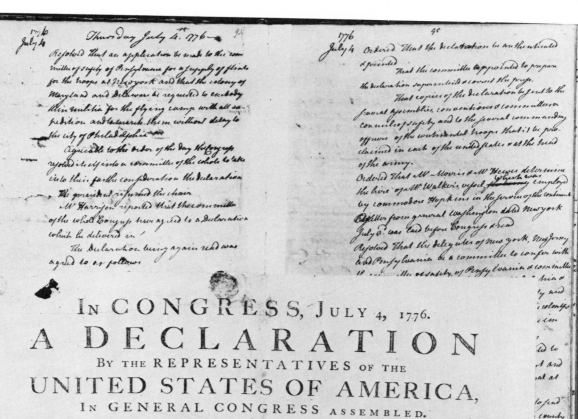

IN CONGRESS, JULY 4, 1776.

A DECLARATION

BY THE REPRESENTATIVES OF THE

UNITED STATES OF AMERICA,

IN GENERAL CONGRESS ASSEMBLED.

WHEN in the Course of human Events, it becomes necessary for one People to dissolve the Political Bands which have connected them with another, and to assume among the Powers of the Earth, the separate and equal Station to which the Laws of Nature and of Nature's God entitle them, a decent Respect to the Opinions of Mankind requires that they should declare the causes which impel them to the Separation.

We hold these Truths to be self-evident, that all Men are created equal, that they are endowed by their Creator with certain unalienable Rights, that among these are Life, Liberty, and the Pursuit of Happiness—That to secure these Rights, Governments are instituted among Men, deriving their just Powers from the Consent of the Governed, that whenever any Form of Government becomes destructive of these Ends, it is the Right of the People to alter or to abolish it, and to institute new Government, laying its Foundation on such Principles, and organizing its Powers in such Form, as to them shall seem most likely to effect their Safety and Happiness. Prudence, indeed, will dictate that Governments long established should not be changed for light and transient Causes; and accordingly all Experience hath shewn, that Mankind are more disposed to suffer, while Evils are sufferable, than to right themselves by abolishing the Forms to which they are accustomed. But when a long Train of Abuses and Usurpations, pursuing invariably the same Object, evinces a Design to reduce them under absolute Despotism, it is their Right, it is their Duty, to throw off such Government, and to provide new Guards for their future Security. Such has been the patient Sufferance of these Colonies; and such is now the Necessity which constrains them to alter their former Systems of Government. The History of the present King of Great-Britain is a History of repeated Injuries and Usurpations, all having in direct Object the Establishment of an absolute Tyranny over these States. To prove this, let Facts be submitted to a candid World.

He has refused his Assent to Laws, the most wholesome and necessary for the public Good.

He has forbidden his Governors to pass Laws of immediate and pressing Importance, unless suspended in their Operation till his Assent should be obtained; and when so suspended, he has utterly neglected to attend to them.

He has refused to pass other Laws for the Accommodation of large Districts of People, unless those People would relinquish the Right of Representation in the Legislature, a Right inestimable to them, and formidable to Tyrants only.

He has called together Legislative Bodies at Places unusual, uncomfortable, and distant from the Depository of their public Records, for the sole Purpose of fatiguing them into Compliance with his Measures.

He has dissolved Representative Houses repeatedly, for opposing with manly Firmness his Invasions on the Rights of the People.

He has refused for a long Time, after such Dissolutions, to cause others to be elected; whereby the Legislative Powers, incapable of Annihilation, have returned to the People at large for their exercise; the State remaining in the mean time exposed to all the Dangers of Invasion from without, and Convulsions within.

He has endeavoured to prevent the Population of these States; for that Purpose obstructing the Laws for Naturalization of Foreigners; refusing to pass others to encourage their Migrations hither, and raising the Conditions of new Appropriations of Lands.

He has obstructed the Administration of Justice, by refusing his Assent to Laws for establishing Judiciary Powers.

He has made Judges dependent on his Will alone, for the Tenure of their Offices, and the Amount and Payment of their Salaries.

He has erected a Multitude of new Offices, and sent hither Swarms of Officers to harrass our People, and eat out their Substance.

He has kept among us, in Times of Peace, Standing Armies, without the consent of our Legislatures.

He has affected to render the Military independent of and superior to the Civil Power.

He has combined with others to subject us to a Jurisdiction foreign to our Constitution, and unacknowledged by our Laws; giving his Assent to their Acts of pretended Legislation:

For quartering large Bodies of Armed Troops among us:

For protecting them, by a mock Trial, from Punishment for any Murders which they should commit on the Inhabitants of these States:

For cutting off our Trade with all Parts of the World:

For imposing Taxes on us without our Consent:

For depriving us, in many Cases, of the Benefits of Trial by Jury:

For transporting us beyond Seas to be tried for pretended Offences:

For abolishing the free System of English Laws in a neighbouring Province, establishing therein an arbitrary Government, and enlarging its Boundaries, so as to render it at once an Example and fit Instrument for introducing the same absolute Rule into these Colonies:

For taking away our Charters, abolishing our most valuable Laws, and altering fundamentally the Forms of our Governments:

For suspending our own Legislatures, and declaring themselves invested with Power to legislate for us in all Cases whatsoever.

He has abdicated Government here, by declaring us out of his Protection and waging War against us.

He has plundered our Seas, ravaged our Coasts, burnt our Towns, and destroyed the Lives of our People.

He is, at this Time, transporting large Armies of foreign Mercenaries to compleat the Works of Death, Desolation, and Tyranny, already begun with circumstances of Cruelty and Perfidy, scarcely paralleled in the most barbarous Ages, and totally unworthy the Head of a civilized Nation.

He has constrained our fellow Citizens taken Captive on the high Seas to bear Arms against their Country, to become the Executioners of their Friends and Brethren, or to fall themselves by their Hands.

He has excited domestic Insurrections amongst us, and has endeavoured to bring on the Inhabitants of our Frontiers, the merciless Indian Savages, whose known Rule of Warfare, is an undistinguished Destruction, of all Ages, Sexes and Conditions.

In every stage of these Oppressions we have Petitioned for Redress in the most humble Terms: Our repeated Petitions have been answered only by repeated Injury. A Prince, whose Character is thus marked by every act which may define a Tyrant, is unfit to be the Ruler of a free People.

Nor have we been wanting in Attentions to our British Brethren. We have warned them from Time to Time of Attempts by their Legislature to extend an unwarrantable Jurisdiction over us. We have reminded them of the Circumstances of our Emigration and Settlement here. We have appealed to their native Justice and Magnanimity, and we have conjured them by the Ties of our common Kindred to disavow these Usurpations, which, would inevitably interrupt our Connections and Correspondence. They too have been deaf to the Voice of Justice and of Consanguinity.. We must, therefore, acquiesce in the Necessity, which denounces our Separation, and hold them, as we hold the rest of Mankind, Enemies in War, in Peace, Friends.

We, therefore, the Representatives of the UNITED STATES OF AMERICA, in General Congress, Assembled, appealing to the Supreme Judge of the World for the Rectitude of our Intentions, do, in the Name, and by Authority of the good People of these Colonies, solemnly Publish and Declare, That these United Colonies are, and of Right ought to be, FREE AND INDEPENDENT STATES; that they are absolved from all Allegiance to the British Crown, and that all political Connection between them and the State of Great-Britain, is and ought to be totally dissolved; and that as FREE AND INDEPENDENT STATES, they have full Power to levy War, conclude Peace, contract Alliances, establish Commerce, and to do all other Acts and Things which INDEPENDENT STATES may of right do. And for the support of this Declaration, with a firm Reliance on the Protection of divine Providence, we mutually pledge to each other our Lives, our Fortunes, and our sacred Honor.

Signed by ORDER and in BEHALF of the CONGRESS,

JOHN HANCOCK, PRESIDENT.

ATTEST.
CHARLES THOMSON, SECRETARY.

PHILADELPHIA: PRINTED BY JOHN DUNLAP.

Jefferson remained annoyed at the way his Declaration had been edited. He spent many hours making copies of his version to send to Virginia friends to show them what Congress had done to the document. He sent copies to Richard Henry Lee; to the president of the Virginia convention, Edmund Pendleton; to his mentor George Wythe (see page 94); to his neighbor, the Italian, Philip Mazzei; and probably to his old friend John Page. In some cases, he indicated Congress's changes right on the copies. To Richard Henry Lee, he sent a copy of his final draft along with the Dunlap broadside for comparison. "You will judge," he wrote Lee, "whether it is the better or worse for the Critics."

His friends, as writers' friends are wont to do, sympathized with him. Edmund Pendleton thought that the members of Congress had treated the Declaration just as badly as they had Jefferson's draft of the 1775 Declaration of Causes. They had, Pendleton said, changed it "much for the worse."

Lee wrote back that he wished

> sincerely, as well for the honor of Congress, as for that
> of the States, that the Manuscript had not been mangled
> as it is. It is wonderful, and passing pitiful, that the rage
> of change should be so unhappily applied.

Consolingly, he added that the piece was

> in its nature so good, that no Cookery can spoil the Dish
> for the palates of Freemen.

The cookery certainly spoiled the dish for the palate of Thomas Jefferson, who put his draft away and scarcely thought about the Declaration for many years. He did, however, along with a number of other members of Congress, sign an ornately hand-lettered (engrossed) copy on August 2, 1776.

This copy, with the signatures of fifty-five signers, is enshrined in the National Archives in Washington. The engrossing was probably done by one of Secretary Thomson's assistants, Timothy Matlack. Matlack had been assigned the hand-lettering job on July 19, when Congress heard that New York had voted in favor of independence.

The new copy reflected New York's action in its title. The document could now boast that the states were unanimous:

> The unanimous Declaration of the thirteen united States
> of America;

instead of, as before:

A Declaration by the Representatives of the UNITED STATES OF AMERICA in GENERAL CONGRESS ASSEMBLED.

(In none of its official transformations has the document borne the title *Declaration of Independence*.)

In copying the Declaration, Matlack accidentally left out two letters of one word and also an entire word. He had to correct these omissions with carets and interlining:

He has dissolved Represtative Houses . . .

Our repeated petitions have been answered by . . .

He also put an extra *t* in *Brittish*, eliminated all the paragraphing, and used capital letters in a completely haphazard fashion. Dunlap, in following broadside usage, had capitalized almost all the nouns. Matlack capitalized some and not others, following no sort of rule at all.

The signers of the Declaration, fearing hanging, kept their names secret. The engrossed, signed parchment copy was carefully hidden away by Charles Thomson.

Jefferson was not able to leave Philadelphia in mid-August as he planned, because his departure would have left Virginia with less than the minimum number of delegates necessary to represent it in the Continental Congress. Finally, around August 20, Francis Lightfoot Lee (Richard Henry Lee's younger brother) returned to Philadelphia, making the Virginia delegation large enough so that Jefferson could be excused. On Sunday, August 25, Jefferson sent Bob Hemings across the river to collect the two horses at Gibson's pasturage, and all four horses were kept at Hiltzheimer's while Jefferson prepared for his departure.

On Tuesday, September 3, he bought some cord for Bob Hemings to use in making fast their baggage. Then he paid Hiltzheimer for stabling his horses, paid Fox the blacksmith for horseshoes, and settled his accounts with Byrne the barber, Binks the saddler, and his landlady, Maria Graff. On his way to Smith's Tavern, he passed people sitting in chairs outside their houses, cooling themselves in the long summer afternoon.

Philadelphia was not all bad. Besides the shops there were the refinements of Smith's: the solid elegance of the wood-paneled walls and the servants—hovering with cheeses, fresh fruits, little cakes and rolls of the German bakers—ever ready to fetch brandy or rum.

Having enjoyed one last, good dinner, Jefferson joined Bob Hemings and headed for the Schuylkill ferry. Each was on horseback, and they led the two other horses with their packs: a tall, sandy-haired aristocrat, never straighter than when in the saddle, and a slender, dark-haired slave, going home to their family in Virginia.

Right: *This engrossed copy is the famous one signed by the "signers." It is enshrined in the National Archives in Washington.* (Library of Congress)

Timothy Matlack seems to have had trouble getting the long title on one line. It looks as if, by the time he had finished the word Declaration, *he realized he had been writing too large. To fit the rest of the title on one line he had to make* of the thirteen united *so much smaller than the rest of the title that the name of the new country was distorted into*

united STATES of AMERICA.

He copied unalienable *from the Dunlap broadside, with the result that this spelling became fixed in all future copies. He also left out a few letters and words that he had to insert between lines. Most of the fifty-five signers affixed their names to the Declaration on August 2, others did so weeks afterward, some as late as November.*

In CONGRESS, July 4, 1776.

The unanimous Declaration of the thirteen united States of America.

When in the Course of human events it becomes necessary for one people to dissolve the political bands which have connected them with another, and to assume among the powers of the earth, the separate and equal station to which the Laws of Nature and of Nature's God entitle them, a decent respect to the opinions of mankind requires that they should declare the causes which impel them to the separation. — We hold these truths to be self-evident, that all men are created equal, that they are endowed by their Creator with certain unalienable Rights, that among these are Life, Liberty and the pursuit of Happiness. — That to secure these rights, Governments are instituted among Men, deriving their just powers from the consent of the governed, — That whenever any Form of Government becomes destructive of these ends, it is the Right of the People to alter or to abolish it, and to institute new Government, laying its foundation on such principles and organizing its powers in such form, as to them shall seem most likely to effect their Safety and Happiness. Prudence, indeed, will dictate that Governments long established should not be changed for light and transient causes; and accordingly all experience hath shewn, that mankind are more disposed to suffer, while evils are sufferable, than to right themselves by abolishing the forms to which they are accustomed. But when a long train of abuses and usurpations, pursuing invariably the same Object evinces a design to reduce them under absolute Despotism, it is their right, it is their duty, to throw off such Government, and to provide new Guards for their future security. — Such has been the patient sufferance of these Colonies; and such is now the necessity which constrains them to alter their former Systems of Government. The history of the present King of Great Britain is a history of repeated injuries and usurpations, all having in direct object the establishment of an absolute Tyranny over these States. To prove this, let Facts be submitted to a candid world. —

He has refused his Assent to Laws, the most wholesome and necessary for the public good. — He has forbidden his Governors to pass Laws of immediate and pressing importance, unless suspended in their operation till his Assent should be obtained; and when so suspended, he has utterly neglected to attend to them. — He has refused to pass other Laws for the accommodation of large districts of people, unless those people would relinquish the right of Representation in the Legislature, a right inestimable to them and formidable to tyrants only. — He has called together legislative bodies at places unusual, uncomfortable, and distant from the depository of their Public Records, for the sole purpose of fatiguing them into compliance with his measures. — He has dissolved Representative Houses repeatedly, for opposing with manly firmness his invasions on the rights of the people. — He has refused for a long time, after such dissolutions, to cause others to be elected; whereby the Legislative powers, incapable of Annihilation, have returned to the People at large for their exercise; the State remaining in the mean time exposed to all the dangers of invasion from without, and convulsions within. — He has endeavoured to prevent the population of these States; for that purpose obstructing the Laws for Naturalization of Foreigners; refusing to pass others to encourage their migrations hither, and raising the conditions of new Appropriations of Lands. — He has obstructed the Administration of Justice, by refusing his Assent to Laws for establishing Judiciary powers. — He has made Judges dependent on his Will alone, for the tenure of their offices, and the amount and payment of their salaries. — He has erected a multitude of New Offices, and sent hither swarms of Officers to harrass our people, and eat out their substance. — He has kept among us, in times of peace, Standing Armies without the Consent of our legislatures. — He has affected to render the Military independent of and superior to the Civil power. — He has combined with others to subject us to a jurisdiction foreign to our constitution, and unacknowledged by our laws; giving his Assent to their Acts of pretended Legislation: — For Quartering large bodies of armed troops among us: — For protecting them, by a mock Trial, from punishment for any Murders which they should commit on the Inhabitants of these States: — For cutting off our Trade with all parts of the world: — For imposing Taxes on us without our Consent: — For depriving us in many cases, of the benefits of Trial by jury: — For transporting us beyond Seas to be tried for pretended offences — For abolishing the free System of English Laws in a neighbouring Province, establishing therein an Arbitrary government, and enlarging its Boundaries so as to render it at once an example and fit instrument for introducing the same absolute rule into these Colonies: — For taking away our Charters, abolishing our most valuable Laws, and altering fundamentally the Forms of our Governments: — For suspending our own Legislatures, and declaring themselves invested with power to legislate for us in all cases whatsoever. — He has abdicated Government here, by declaring us out of his Protection and waging War against us. — He has plundered our seas, ravaged our Coasts, burnt our towns, and destroyed the lives of our people. — He is at this time transporting large Armies of foreign Mercenaries to compleat the works of death, desolation and tyranny, already begun with circumstances of Cruelty & perfidy scarcely paralleled in the most barbarous ages, and totally unworthy the Head of a civilized nation. — He has constrained our fellow Citizens taken Captive on the high Seas to bear Arms against their country, to become the executioners of their friends and Brethren, or to fall themselves by their Hands. — He has excited domestic insurrections amongst us, and has endeavoured to bring on the inhabitants of our frontiers, the merciless Indian Savages, whose known rule of warfare, is an undistinguished destruction of all ages, sexes and conditions. In every stage of these Oppressions We have Petitioned for Redress in the most humble terms: Our repeated Petitions have been answered only by repeated injury. A Prince, whose character is thus marked by every act which may define a Tyrant, is unfit to be the ruler of a free people. Nor have We been wanting in attentions to our British brethren. We have warned them from time to time of attempts by their legislature to extend an unwarrantable jurisdiction over us. We have reminded them of the circumstances of our emigration and settlement here. We have appealed to their native justice and magnanimity, and we have conjured them by the ties of our common kindred to disavow these usurpations, which, would inevitably interrupt our connections and correspondence. They too have been deaf to the voice of justice and of consanguinity. We must, therefore, acquiesce in the necessity, which denounces our Separation, and hold them, as we hold the rest of mankind, Enemies in War, in Peace Friends. —

We, therefore, the Representatives of the united States of America, in General Congress, Assembled, appealing to the Supreme Judge of the world for the rectitude of our intentions, do, in the Name, and by Authority of the good People of these Colonies, solemnly publish and declare, That these United Colonies are, and of Right ought to be Free and Independent States; that they are Absolved from all Allegiance to the British Crown, and that all political connection between them and the State of Great Britain, is and ought to be totally dissolved; and that as Free and Independent States, they have full Power to levy War, conclude Peace, contract Alliances, establish Commerce, and to do all other Acts and Things which Independent States may of right do. — And for the support of this Declaration, with a firm reliance on the protection of divine Providence, we mutually pledge to each other our Lives, our Fortunes and our sacred Honor.

John Hancock

Button Gwinnett
Lyman Hall
Geo Walton.

W.m Hooper
Joseph Hewes,
John Penn

Edward Rutledge.

Tho.s Heyward Jun.r
Thomas Lynch Jun.r
Arthur Middleton

Rob.t Morris
Benjamin Rush
Benj.a Franklin
John Morton
Geo Clymer
Ja.s Smith.
Geo. Taylor
James Wilson
Geo. Ross
Caesar Rodney
Geo Read
Tho M:Kean

Samuel Chase
W.m Paca
Thos. Stone
Charles Carroll of Carrollton

George Wythe
Richard Henry Lee
Th Jefferson
Benj.a Harrison
Th.s Nelson jr.
Francis Lightfoot Lee
Carter Braxton

W.m Floyd
Phil. Livingston
Fran.s Lewis
Lewis Morris

Rich.d Stockton
Jn.o Witherspoon
Fra.s Hopkinson
John Hart
Abra Clark

Josiah Bartlett
W.m Whipple
Sam.l Adams
John Adams
Rob.t Treat Paine
Elbridge Gerry
Step. Hopkins
William Ellery
Roger Sherman
Sam.el Huntington
W.m Williams
Oliver Wolcott
Matthew Thornton

CHAPTER FIFTEEN

The Spirit of Revolution

Few state papers outlive their occasions. The first page of the Declaration of Independence survives today because of the spirit of revolution it expresses. The principles held self-evident by Jefferson in 1776 were destined to be held self-evident by almost all mankind.

Words have their own existence. The ideas in Jefferson's Declaration were not as familiar as the members of Congress thought. By shifting the emphasis slightly, Jefferson gave them a new shape. When the patriots cited John Locke, their attention was on the *rights* they by nature all possessed, the rights of those who were "free, equal and independent."

Heeding inner voices and obscure visions, Jefferson plucked *equal* from the interlacings of *free* and *independent* and put the idea of equality first, before freedom and independence. When he gave as the first of the "self-evident" truths that *all men are created equal*, he made equality the foundation of his argument. The idea that *all men are created equal* became the heart of the American vision, a vision that is changing the world to this day. It became, as President Lincoln would note in 1861, "a standard maxim for free society . . . a stumbling block to all those who in after times might seek to turn a free people back into the hateful path of despotism.

"And more [as Lincoln continued], not just an affirmation of American liberty, but hope to all the world for all future time. It . . . gave promise that in due time the weights would be lifted from the shoulders of all men, and that all should have an equal chance."

Jefferson was riding the wave of the future. The American Revolution did not merely end two centuries of colonization of the northwestern shore of the Atlantic. It began a new era in which the power of kings would be replaced by that of elected officials, and the old aristocracies of land would give way to new aristocracies of trade.

The American Revolutionary War was the very first anticolonial rebellion. It was the first time that a small group of determined people, oppressed by distant masters, won independence. It was basically a guerrilla war in which a small number of poorly armed natives was able, with the help of powerful friends, to defeat a much larger, better-equipped force. It was the model for all the struggles for independence that have since taken place in Latin America, Africa, and Asia.

The spirit of revolution expressed in the second paragraph of the Declaration has inspired the births of many nations. True to its revolutionary heritage, the United States of America often encouraged the independence of others. False to that same heritage (and its government, as Jefferson feared, grown overpowerful), the United States has increasingly found itself helping other governments, old and new, to oppress their people. If Jefferson's faith in the wisdom and virtue of ordinary men and women remains to be justified, "the people" nevertheless continue to strive for a chance to govern themselves.

Notes

1. How Jefferson was selected to write the Declaration. (page 12)

No one seems to have recorded at the time the workings of the five-man committee appointed to write the Declaration. Many years later, when the document had assumed historical stature and questions began being asked about it, both Adams and Jefferson set down their recollections—Adams in his autobiography (1805), and again in a letter to Timothy Pickering (1822); Jefferson in a letter to James Madison (1823). Because the two accounts differ in some respects, anyone trying to reconstruct these events must choose between them. Where the two men principally differ is in the manner in which Jefferson was selected to draft the Declaration. Adams says that he and Jefferson were appointed to a subcommittee of two to write it, and that he then persuaded Jefferson to do it alone. Jefferson denied that there ever was a subcommittee and asserted that there never was any question but that he would do the draft.

Which story are we to follow? What we know of the practices of Congress supports Jefferson. As the member who received the most votes, the Virginian automatically would have headed the five-man committee. As head of the committee, unless he appointed someone else, he would have been expected to draft the document.

2. Who saw the Declaration first, Adams or Franklin? (page 45)

Professor Carl Becker of Cornell, the first to subject the Rough Draft and Adams's copy to careful analysis, concluded that Franklin saw it first. His decision was based on the fact that changes made by Franklin were incorporated into the copy that John Adams prepared. Becker mentions two of Franklin's changes that appear in the Adams copy. About the first of these—the changes made by Franklin to page 2, line 22—he clearly was in error, as these do not appear in the Adams copy. The second case is more complicated. In the Rough Draft, Jefferson attributes the change on page 1, line 23, from *to arbitrary power* to *under absolute Despotism* (see page 66) to Franklin. In Adams's copy, this appears as *under absolute power*, which corresponds neither to the original wording nor to the complete change as attributed to Franklin. Becker explained this by saying that either Adams had made an error in copying or two changes had been made here, at two different times: first to *under absolute power*; then to *under absolute Despotism*. If both changes had been made by Franklin, even at different times, then this would indeed be evidence that Franklin had seen the document first. However, Professor Julian Boyd of Princeton points out that, on close examination, *under absolute* appears to have been written by a different hand than *Despotism; under absolute* appears to be in Jefferson's handwriting, and *Despotism* in Franklin's. If this is so, then Jefferson changed the first two words, making the expression *under absolute power*, which is just the way Adams copied it. Then, later, when Franklin saw the document, he changed *power* to *Despotism*. This destroys the only basis remaining for Becker's belief that Franklin saw the Declaration first.

We still must explain, however, why Jefferson attributed the entire three-word change to Franklin, and not just the alteration to *Despotism*. As Jefferson's marginal notes on the Rough Draft, attributing sources of changes, were made many years after the event, his memory could have been faulty. He should have placed the + mark in front of *Despotism* instead of in front of *under*.

3. Bob Hemings. (pgs. 2, 4, 16, 19, 25, 26, . . . etc.)

It is a curious fact that no history of these events has previously identified the young man who was with Jefferson while he composed the Declaration. The evidence has long been available. Indeed, as long ago as 1906, J. H. Hazelton, in his lengthy study *The Declaration of Independence, Its History*, reprinted (pages 454–456) in full the notes from Jefferson's 1776 account book that refer to Bob. The young slave is given passing, first-name reference in just one book, Dumas Malone's *Jefferson the Virginian* (Little, Brown,

1948). At any time, anyone troubling to examine Jefferson's Farm Book could have discovered that he possessed only one slave named Bob: Bob Hemings, born in 1762, and inherited by Jefferson's wife, Martha, from her father, John Wayles.

Bob Hemings's probable ancestry is given in the memoirs of Isaac Jefferson, one of Thomas's slaves; and there are many references to him in correspondence between Jefferson and his daughter, Martha Jefferson Randolph. Bob seems to have been an especially favored house slave. He was trusted to travel alone, even between Monticello and Philadelphia, and appointed to drive his master's fast phaeton carriage. Bob obtained his freedom at the end of 1794, when he was thirty-two years old, but he had to pay for it. What happened was that Bob impregnated a house slave owned by a man in Richmond, Dr. George Frederick Strauss. Jefferson manumitted Bob, but made Dr. Strauss pay for him—a sum which, presumably, Bob repaid to the doctor out of his wages. Jefferson resented losing Bob, who felt compelled to explain to Martha Randolph, when she visited him, that he "could not have quitted [Jefferson] to live with any person but [my] wife." Some time afterward, Bob lost his hand in a gun accident. He died in 1819.

4. Jefferson and the Scotch "mercenaries." (pgs. 20, 32)

There are several reasons for believing that Jefferson included Scots among the mercenaries referred to on his work sheet for the next-to-last paragraph, as a result of hearing a letter read to Congress on the morning of June 18. The letter, dispatched to General Washington by General Artemas Ward in Massachusetts, on June 9, contained the following information:

"yesterday a ship from Scotland was taken and brought into Marblehead by the Continental armed schooners Warren and Lee. She had on board a company of Highlanders consisting of 100 privates, one Captain, 3 sub-alterns and 2 volunteers. They inform that 32 sail of transports came out with them under convoy of a frigate of 32 guns, with 3000 Highlanders on board a l bound for Boston. . ."
Ward's letter reached Washington, in New York, about a week later, on the 16th or early on the 17th, and was forwarded by Washington to Congress, which heard it on the 18th during Hancock's daily oral reading of the mail.

The reasons for thinking that the letter caused Jefferson to add his reference to Scots as mercenaries to the next-to-last paragraph, are as follows:

a) He and other members of Congress had known for more than a month that Scots were included among the King's troops. The secret message, delivered by George Merchant, listed all the regiments raised in Britain and Scotland, in addition to the German troops. Similar lists, reprinted from British newspapers, also appeared in the Philadelphia press.

b) References that followed receipt of the news included the Scots among the King's troops, not among the mercenaries. For example, a resolution passed by Congress mentioned "the whole power of that kingdom aided by foreign mercenaries."

c) As a result of the Act of Union (1707), Scotland and Britain were joined. Scots, therefore, on no account could be called either foreigners or mercenaries.

d) In his preamble to a proposed Virginia constitution, written no later than June 13, Jefferson spoke simply of "foreign mercenaries."

Why did Jefferson write *Scotch and foreign mercenaries* for the first time on his work sheet for the penultimate paragraph? The Scots, whose capture was announced by General Ward, were the first members of the 30,000-man invasion force to appear on these shores. This was alarming news —the huge army was almost upon America! Shocked by this news, and wishing somehow to refer to it in the document he was writing, Jefferson inserted the words *Scotch and.*

June 18, the date Jefferson heard General Ward's letter, thus becomes the earliest date on which he could have made this alteration on his work sheet. This means that he could not have finished his original draft of the Declaration before this day.

The injudiciousness of this change—the Scots were no more "mercenaries" than any others of the King's troops—was brought home to Jefferson when Congress went over the Declaration. James Wilson, John Witherspoon, and Thomas McKean, three Scots, were the severest of his editors. As Jefferson was to note many years later, "The words 'Scotch and other foreign auxiliaries' [Jefferson misremembered the word, probably because of lingering pain over the incident] excited the ire of a gentleman or two of that country. . . . altho' the offensive expressions were immediately yielded, these gentlemen continued their depredation on other parts of the instrument."

Bibliography

Books about the Declaration of Independence

The Declaration of Independence: A Study in the History of Political Ideas, by Carl Becker. New York: Harcourt Brace and Company, 1922.

The Declaration of Independence: The Evolution of the Text, by Julian P. Boyd. Princeton, N.J.: Princeton University Press, 1945.

The Declaration of Independence—Its History, by John H. Hazelton. New York: Dodd Mead, 1906.

Writings of Thomas Jefferson

The Papers of Thomas Jefferson, Vol. 1. Julian P. Boyd, editor. Princeton, N.J.: Princeton University Press, 1950.

Thomas Jefferson's Farm Book, with Commentary and Relevant Extracts from Other Writings. Edwin M. Betts, editor. Princeton, N.J.: Princeton University Press, 1953.

Thomas Jefferson's Account Book, 1776. Unpublished manuscript. Boston: Massachusetts Historical Society.

Jefferson's Contemporaries

The Adams Papers: Diary and Autobiography of John Adams, Vols. 2, 3. Lyman H. Butterfield, editor. Cambridge, Mass.: Belknap Press of Harvard University, 1961.

Letters of John Adams Addressed to His Wife, Vol. 1. Charles F. Adams, editor. Boston: Little, Brown, 1841.

Life and Writings of John Dickinson, Vol. 1. Memoirs of the Historical Society of Pennsylvania, Vol. 13. Philadelphia: Historical Society of Pennsylvania, 1891.

Benjamin Franklin, by Carl Van Doren. New York: Viking Press, 1938.

General Background

American Archives, 4th Series, Vol. 6. Peter Force, editor. Washington: M. St. Clair Clark & P. Force, 1846.

Bulletin, Pennsylvania Historical Society, January 1905, Robert Edge Pine, by Charles Hart.

Journals of the Continental Congress, 1775, 1776. W. C. Ford and others, editors. Washington, 1904–1937.

Documents of American History, 7th ed. Henry S. Commager, editor. New York: Appleton-Century-Crofts, 1967.

Dictionary of American Biography. Allen Johnson and Dumas Malone, editors. New York: Charles Scribner's Sons, 1928–1944.

Historic Philadelphia, *Transactions of the American Philosophical Society*, New Series, Vol. 43, Part 1, Philadelphia, 1953.

Philadelphia. American Guide Series, compiled by the Federal Writers' Project, WPA for the Commonwealth of Pennsylvania. Philadelphia: William Penn Association, 1937.

Jefferson and Monticello, by Paul Wilstock. New York: Doubleday Page, 1925.

Jefferson the Virginian, by Dumas Malone. Boston: Little, Brown, 1948.

Thomas Jefferson: An Intimate History, by Fawn M. Brodie. New York: W. W. Norton, 1974.

On Revolution, by Hannah Arendt. New York: Viking Press, 1963.

The Violent Men, by Cornelia Meigs. New York: The Macmillan Company, 1949.

A Transaction of Free Men, by David Hawke. New York: Charles Scribner's Sons, 1964.

The Spirit of '76, Vol. 1. H. S. Commager & R. B. Morris, editors. Indianapolis: Bobbs-Merrill, 1958.

An Answer to the Declaration of the American Congress, by Jonathan Lind. London: Cadell, Walter & Sewell, 1776.

Newspapers

Pennsylvania Gazette, June, July 1776.

Articles

"New Light on Jefferson and His Great Task," Julian P. Boyd, *New York Times* Magazine, April 13, 1947.

Index

Italicized numbers refer to illustrations and/or captions.

Date Due

MAR 3 0 1987		
APR 2 8 1987		
NO 2 6 '92		
AP 1 9 '93		
NOV 01 1993		
APR 1 8 1994		
NOV 1 0 1994		
DEC 1 2 97		